Many Lives

of

Maryanne

Maryanne Chambers Gilmore

Maryanne Chambers Gilmore

Ameba Publishing
Durant, Oklahoma

The Many Lives of Maryanne

Published by:
Ameba Publishing
P.O. Box 383
Durant, OK 74702
Phone (580) 931-3332
www.amebapublishing.com

ISBN, print edition   978-0-9744827-1-2

Printed in the United States of America

INTRODUCTION

Just the Facts Ma'am!

When I was asked to write a book about my life most recently, I just smiled. It is all too easy to ramble about events and emotions. What's hard is just sticking to the facts.

The last time I attempted to record feelings for my sons was in the early 1980's, and it was a disaster. First of all, I thought I was dying, and hurried to get it all on paper. But worse, I included too much extra baggage. It scared my boys to death. Reading it in later years, I do realize that it was depressing.

This book will not be the story of my life, down to the minute detail. As Jody Vaughan once told me, if I ever wrote that story, it would have to be as a novel, because nobody would ever believe that it was true!

Yeah, it's been an experience....And it ain't over yet! If I live long enough, I might get around to recording it all. But not now.... this one is G rated, for all the world to see...which might make it a little boring, but it's my intention to jot down the most important events, and expound only on the people most closely involved in this adventure called LIFE.

APPRECIATION

During my quest for a publisher, it was my good fortune to find Kathy Carpenter with Ameba Publishing in Durant, Oklahoma. She has worked personally and tirelessly to help me bring my book to reality. A sincere "Thank You" to my newest friend, Kathy.

ACKNOWLEDGEMENT

Finally, after all this work is done, I understand why authors have to recognize so many people. No work is ever that of one person alone, but must rely on the aid of others.

My youngest son, Billy, and my oldest granddaughter, Angel, both prodded me until I finally began the book. I'm not sure I owe them any thanks for that!

My big brother, Tommy Lee, and sister Charlotte supported my efforts to record memories of our childhood, and bragged on me when I needed encouragement.

My friend, Dennis Vaughan, the son of Bill's first boss, helped me through the pipeline years, where we met when he was a child. His memories jogged my own, as I struggled for names and places.

My Bill has been my proof-reader and critic, patiently watching old westerns while I sat at the computer. Sometimes we disagreed, but he allowed me to make my own mistakes.

To all of them, I owe more that I'm willing to admit. But thanks, anyway!

DEDICATION

I intended to dedicate this book to all the people I love. But, there are too many of you. So, instead, I'm dedicating it to all of those who love Me!

That cuts the list down considerably!

BOOK 1

Table of Contents
Book I
Childhood Through My Teens

Chapter:

...another mouth to feed...

Chapter 1

I WAS BORN...

.... then suddenly, everything went blank!

That's one of my favorite jokes from my childhood. Just never thought I'd have the opportunity to use it in a book! But hey, it fits! I waited too long to remember every important item. But I do remember being told that I WAS BORN..... February 5, 1932 at Skellytown, Texas, the home of Skelly Oil Company.

Being the last of eight children couldn't possibly be a very welcome position. But Rosetta Stringfellow Chambers, and Robert Burton Chambers, accepted me into the world. Maybe if abortion had been available and acceptable back then, I might not be here. [Thank God, it wasn't!!!]

But if I was not wanted, I certainly can't say I was not loved. It took me a few decades to realize just how much I was loved. The mere fact that the older children didn't drown me is evidence that somebody must have loved me.

Lillie Ruth was the first child of Mama and Daddy. She was twenty two years old when I was born. Their second was a son, Cecil Louis, who died in an epidemic at age 7, on Christmas Eve, 1918. The folks were visiting in Wewoka, Oklahoma, and buried him there on Christmas Day.

Glen Frank was next, followed by Nina June, and Roberta Marie. Then came Thomas Lee and Charlotte Jo.

Oh yeah, I'm sure they all were excited about adding another mouth to feed, and finding space for a new baby.......... during the Great Depression.

...life would imitate
that of my mother...

Chapter 2

MAMA AND DADDY

What little I know about the background of my Mother and my Father was learned by listening to stories throughout my life with them. On their 50th anniversary, Glen made a tape recording of them telling about their wedding. It was a glorified version, and I always wished they had told the truth. But I came to realize, as Bill and I lived together for so many, many years, that we do forget the bad, and the good becomes the only truth.

Mama was born September 26, 1892, into a relatively wealthy home, in comparison to the life she would live with Daddy. The pictures of her as a young girl show elegant clothing, and a child obviously well cared for. She had one living sister, Aunt Nora. They lived on a farm, but it was a very nice home.

Daddy was born May 24, 1886, the youngest child of aged parents who both had children from other marriages. His mother, Mary Jane Hamilton Campbell Haning Chambers, had lost two husbands, and at least one adult son. His father, Louis Pearl Chambers, had also lost a wife and a son. Together, they raised her grandson and granddaughter, Matt and Alice Campbell, and his grandson, Rupert Chambers, along with their crippled son, Sam, Uncle Charley, and my daddy. All their other children were adults, with families of their own.

Daddy was 23 when he married Mama and she was 16. No doubt he had been responsible for himself for several years. Certainly, he had already lived an interesting life, moving around Oklahoma, Colorado and New Mexico as a ranch hand. At one point, he was a deputy for Pat Garrett, years after that famous man had captured Billy the Kid.

Daddy had been engaged to a girl who died. Her name was Lillie. When I was a teen-ager at Iowa Park, Mama related a dream to me that Daddy had experienced the night before. He had woke her, and told her that he had seen his Lillie, coming down the side of a hill. She had aged, just as he had, but they knew each other. They sat down and talked for a long time. He told her about his family and everything that had happened in his life since she had died. She was happy for him. Then, she just walked back up the hill and disappeared.

In the morning, when Mama and Daddy got up, they discovered that it was the anniversary of the girl's death.

Mother also had a previous boy friend. His name was Finas Carter. She was very much in love with him. I was 16 when she told me that. It made me extremely angry with her, to think that she could have loved anybody besides my daddy. In my immaturity, I had no idea that people can love more than one person. Mama's heart was broken when another girl got pregnant, and Finas was charged with being the father.

He proved that other boys had been with the girl, and was not held responsible. But in the very early 1900's, it was a disgrace for a boy just as much as for a girl. He left town. I'm sure that even if he had stayed, Mama would never have overcome his act of unfaithfulness to her.

There's no doubt that Mama and Daddy had each told the other about their heart breaking experiences, and that made them close. In addition, it appears that Grandpa was mean to Mama. Maybe she was as much a problem as a teen-ager as I was. Certainly, Grandpa had valid reason for not wanting her dating a 23 year old man. But whatever the case, the two of them ran away together, by horse and buggy.

They went to Mangum, Oklahoma, where Daddy had an uncle with his name, Robert B.Chambers. They got married January 29, 1909.

I can only imagine the cultural shock Mama experienced, going from a secure home, into a 'dug-out', a structure with dirt floors, and walls and roof built into the side of a hill. Within a couple of months, she was pregnant with her first child. After Lillie was born, Grandpa forgave her, and they returned to Hammon to visit her parents.

I adored Mama and Daddy. Much of my life would imitate that of my mother.

...give him that sandwich...

Chapter 3

THE DEPRESSION

While the depression wasn't easy on our family, we didn't suffer like many others, due to the fact that Daddy always had a job with Skelly Oil Company. We had food from a garden, and shelter. We always lived in company houses, and had gas for heat, and electric lights. There was cold running water in the kitchen.

All those things were signs of affluence back then. Everybody had cardboard in their shoes, when the soles wore through, so we didn't know we were poor. We certainly never experienced any of the hardships of the many who had to go through a soup line for a meal, or find a place to sleep at night.

In recent years, Lillie related a story to me that brought the reality of the depression home to me.

She was working in Borger, boarding with a family there, when I was a baby. [I guess I had better explain that "boarding" means renting a room, and getting meals with it.]

One day, she had just fixed a sandwich with the last bread and meat available. There was a knock on the back door, and a man told her he had just gotten off the freight train, and he wondered if she had anything for him to eat. She told him he could have the sandwich she had just fixed, because she had eaten something that morning, and could get by.

Just then there was a knock at the front door. When she got to it, there was a little boy, about 12, standing there, crying. The man at the back door looked through the house and saw the boy. He told Lillie, "That's the kid that was on the train with me. He's all by himself. You give him that sandwich. I'll find something to eat later."

THAT was the depression.

...this is Bob's baby...

Chapter 4

SKELLY OIL COMPANY

Daddy was one of four men working for W.G. Skelly, before he formed his company, who stayed with him. Except for a brief time when he took the family to New Mexico for Lillie's health, Daddy worked for Skelly Oil Company from the very first day of operation.

In 1920, when Roberta was born, my parents were living at Clara, Texas. Their closest friends were George and Nellie Leath. George was also a Skelly man. They had a large family, too. When Daddy took his family to New Mexico, the Leaths went out to visit them.... a visit that all of them remembered through the years. Both Clara, Texas, and the Leath family, became a part of my life, in later years.

As a small child, while we were living in Wynona, I recall personal contact between Daddy and W.G. Skelly on a somewhat regular basis. I remember visits to the office in Tulsa, where we were welcomed as family.

Most of all, I remember one special company picnic, bigger than the county fairs I had been to.... a carnival-like setting, with everything a child could want. Then, Mr. Skelly came by, picked me up and carried me all around the picnic, telling everybody he met, "This is Bob's baby..."

When Tommy returned from WWII, he also became a Skelly man, staying until he retired. By then, it had become Getty Oil Company... but to us, it will forever be Skelly.

Bill and I were living in Cleveland, Oklahoma when Cecil was a baby. Daddy wanted us to go to Tulsa to see his old friend, one of the original four, who was in charge of hiring. Daddy wanted us to be part of the Skelly family, too. So, we went to the Skelly main office, in Tulsa.

I thought I'd never forget that man's name, so familiar to me as a child. But it's gone from my memory. That day, he took us to lunch. At one point, he looked at me and said, "I owe my job to your daddy."

He told me that my daddy was supposed to have had his position, but refused it, saying he couldn't work in an office.

That refusal probably upset Mama. It forever changed the life she would live from that which it could have been.

And me? How would I have lived my young life as the child of a Skelly official? All I know is, my daddy was perfect, and if he had rather work in the plants, that's exactly what he should have done.

Chapter 5

WYNONA

When I was about 2 years old, Daddy was transferred to the Skelly plant at Wynona, Oklahoma. Lillie was already married to Berry Barnes, and stayed near Skellytown, where she became the Post Mistress. A couple of years later, they had Joetta, and I became an aunt, at the ripe old age of 4. Glen was already out of high school when we moved there, and was working in Pawhuska. But he lived at home until he married Marvel.

The houses in the Skelly camp were all alike, with a living room, two bedrooms, a dining room and kitchen. The bedrooms were to one side, and the other three rooms were in a row, so that you looked from the front door to the back of the house. Of course, every family had beds in the living room and dining room, until some of the kids left home.

I don't remember where Glen and Tommy slept.... maybe in the living room. Otherwise, it had to have been in the room with Mama and Daddy. Nina and Roberta were teen-agers, and had the other bedroom to themselves. Charlotte and I slept on a day-bed in the dining room.... one at each end, with our feet always kicking each other!

Daddy liked working the midnight shift, going to work at 11pm, and being home all day. We had a ritual that, before he left, he would pick up either Charlotte or me, and put us in the bed with Mama. When it was my turn, I sometimes pretended to be asleep, because I liked for Daddy to carry me and, if I was awake, I thought he would make me walk by myself.

Before we went to bed, Mama gathered all the girls, and we went out to the outhouse together. If it was cold, we all crowded inside, waiting for our turn to pee, pleading for the one sitting down to "Hurry UP!"

The camp was my whole world. All the families watched all the kids. I don't remember all of them, only the ones that we had a lot of contact with. The Culps were our closest friends. Otis [we all called him Bus] was Tommy's best friend.... and remained so from then on through life. Wina Mae and Juanita were near the ages of Roberta and Nina. Then, Mrs. Culp got pregnant when I was about 6, and Mr. Culp ran away with another woman. We all hated him for that.

Mr. Munns was the superintendent at Wynona. They had some boys that we played with. One was Billy. I don't remember the others.

Mr. Cooper was the only man Daddy didn't like. He raised fighting roosters, being mean to them, so that they would fight to the death. So, we didn't visit with that family. But their boy, Ernest, was always around.

We had a dog named Minnie..... and she had 9 puppies.... One of them was Spot, who became Tommy's dog. Well, he allowed the rest of us to love him, too. And Spot was a part of my life from then on, until he died after I was married. I guess he still is, in my heart. I don't remember what happened to Minnie.

My school days began at Wynona. All the kids from the camp gathered together to wait for the school bus. Some carried lunch pails, but Tommy, Charlotte and I didn't, even though there was no cafeteria at school.

When the noon bell rang, we all walked the short way to downtown, and went to the grocery store, with several other families of children. In the back room, each family had the remainder of their bread loaf on a shelf, with other items they might have that didn't perish, such as mustard. As we went in, we picked out our drinks, and got our lunch meat out of the refrigerator, where the grocer had everything labeled. And we were allowed to get a cookie out of the bin. I think this bounty cost our Daddy 25 cents a day for the three of us.

Sometimes, we went to the hamburger joint, [they were not 'shops' back then]. But that cost us 15 cents each. When the hamburgers went up another nickel, that ended those lunches.

After my second grade year, we moved about 10 miles away. Daddy had the opportunity to take over a one-man plant between Wynona and Pawhuska, and he didn't hesitate. It meant he could work his own hours, but was responsible 24 hours a day.

I'm not so sure that Mama appreciated having him under foot all day, at odd times. But she certainly would love living in a single home on a very large plant yard, with no neighbors within at least a half mile.

...just plain drunk!...

Chapter 6

GRANDMA AND GRANDPA

M y grandma and grandpa were my mother's parents. My daddy's folks were old when he was born, so of course, they died before I was born. The only memory I have of them is through pictures, and what I have been told. They are a part of my life only through genealogy, and that is for another book, written by someone else.

Grandma and Grandpa Stringfellow lived in Hammon, Oklahoma, just north of Elk City. I'm sure we didn't make very many trips across the state back then, but there were enough for me to know them. They didn't have an automobile, and never came to our home.

I have very few memories of Grandpa, as he died when I was four. I do remember sitting on their front porch with him, and him telling me to go get his pipe. I went in the house, and got matches. When I got back, he said, "No. I don't need matches. I want my pipe." So, I made another trip, and brought back tobacco. This time, he really scolded me, and yelled, "I said I WANT MY PIPE!!!!!" That time, I got it right.

I have never known if I was just so young that I associated all of those things with his pipe, or if I was daring enough to tease a gruff, old man. Whatever, I didn't do it again!

Another time, Mama and I were on the front porch. We looked out in the street that started up on a hill, led down in front of the house, and continued on to downtown. We saw Grandpa coming down the hill, and watched him stumble and fall. I didn't understand why Mama got mad, and went in the house to tell Grandma, "Well, Daddy's sick again!"

After I grew up, I learned that when somebody said Grandpa was sick, that meant he was just plain DRUNK!

They still owned the farm a short distance from town where they had raised Mama and her only sibling, Aunt Nora. One of the highlights of our trip was always a visit to the farm. We kids enjoyed it, but I'm sure it brought back a lot of memories for Mama.

As an adult, I was told a story about my grandma running away with another man, and Grandpa going after her. It never fit with the Grandma I knew, but then, she wasn't always my grandma.

And those things happened in those days, just as they do now. So it might have happened. It didn't change the woman I loved one iota.

Obviously, they loved each other, in their own way. Grandpa would come in the front door, and yell "Oh, MAGGIE!" And Grandma would yell back, "Oh, JIGGS!" Maggie and Jiggs were cartoon characters in my childhood, and for Grandma and Grandpa to call themselves by those names meant they had to have fun together.

I don't remember anything about Grandpa's death, except his burial. It was the first time I had ever seen a box being put into the ground with a person in it. I wondered how my Grandpa was going to get out. I must not have worried about it long, since it didn't mess me up for life!

After Grandpa died, it was just "going to Grandma's house!" Oh, my goodness, I could write a book about Grandma! She was everything a grandma could be to a little girl.

Each time we went, as soon as she saw our car pull into the driveway, she came dancing off the porch, down the steps, clapping and twirling around and around, all the way to the car. It was a ritual that never ended, as long as her body was able to dance. I've always been grateful that Bill got to see it, when we went for a visit after we married.

When I was a little older, and we had moved to Texas, I got to ride the train from Burburnett to Hammon each summer to spend some time with Grandma. That's one of my fondest memories.

We would sit on that front porch, and people passing would always come and sit a while, or at least yell at us from the street. She knew everybody, and we would walk down that hill to town, going into all the stores, where the people were happy to see us, and we were just old friends.

Even as a child, I had a knack for fixing hair. Grandma always loved for me to put her hair on rollers, and comb it out before we went to Church. But, I know I loved doing it more than she did.

Grandma died in 1956, after a long ordeal with skin cancer that took her right ear completely off. I was living in Washington State. I was ill and couldn't come home for her funeral. It devastated me.

The high point in my young life always was going to Grandma's house.

...that swim across Uncle Charley's lake...

Chapter 7

UNCLE CHARLEY'S LAKE

It wasn't really Uncle Charley's Lake, but we thought it was. When we went to Grandma's house, it was a relatively short distance on to McClain, Texas, near Shamrock to see Daddy's only living brother.

There was this beautiful, huge, open house on the water, with screened porches on all sides. We stayed there, at least once, sleeping on the porch in the cool breeze. It was Uncle Charley's too.... or so I thought.

Actually, Uncle Charley was the caretaker of the Country Club property. Obviously, he had arranged for his family to use the facilities, if they were available when we were there.

Uncle Charley did live on the property, in a small house, not big enough to hold all of us. He was divorced, and his only son, George, lived with his mother. I believe her name was Velta, and I'm told she was a beautiful woman.

Maybe that lake wasn't as large as we all remember it to have been, but it was pretty big. Roberta was probably about 16 or so when our entire family was staying in the Country Club House. Somebody told Mama that she was out in the middle of the lake. Mama told Daddy to go get her.... so Daddy got in a boat and rowed out to where Roberta was swimming. He pulled up beside her, and asked if she could make it... She told him she could. So, he just paddled along, letting her finish what she had started.

That story has been a family treasure ever since. We had reason to be proud of Roberta in later years, but nothing ever down-played that swim across Uncle Charley's lake!

Uncle Charley died tragically when his house burned. He had just come in from the grocery store, according to his friends. Evidence seemed to point to arson. Daddy always believed that his only full brother was murdered.

George, Uncle Charley's son, grew up to find a measure of fame as Tex Chambers, training dogs to perform for entertainment. He was on the 'Ed Sullivan Show' that introduced Elvis Presley.

He went to see Mama and Daddy sometime in the 1950's, while I was raising my little boys. He put on a show in the front yard for them, and the other children... and adults.... that passed by. We have always remembered that, and been grateful.

I understand he didn't spend the night with the folks, because Mama wouldn't let his dogs in the house. Mama never let ANY dog in the house!!!

George is still living as I write this. He is in the northeast near Georgia, his daughter who found us a few years ago.

Georgia also found her half-brother, George Jr. Those two have shared our Chambers Family reunions. We have not yet met his other children. But we will.

Chapter 8

THE CAMPBELL FAMILY

Matt Campbell was Daddy and Uncle Charley's nephew, who was raised with them, along with his sister, Alice, and another nephew, Rupert Chambers. Matt's grandmother, Mary Jane, was also my grandmother, which made us first cousins, although he was my daddy's age.

Matt and his wife, Martha, lived next to Uncle Charley, with their very large family. There were 10 children in all. But the only girls I remember were Faye, Mary, Jane, and Alice. Faye was the oldest, but I never knew which of the other three was the youngest of the girls. Then, they had a set of twin boys, just a little younger than me.... Billy and Bobby. Obviously, the others were grown before I was old enough to remember.

Those were the most beautiful girls I had ever seen in my life. That's saying a lot, because I had some beautiful sisters. But the Campbell girls were really gorgeous.

The little twin boys were so shy that they hid, and peeked around the corner of the house at us. But they, too, had the same beautiful eyes as their sisters.

The answer, of course, was that Martha was an Indian woman, and the children all inherited that beauty. We have always affectionately called them our "Indian" cousins. I recently heard them described as "The Ten Little Indians"

Over the years, we have remained in contact with the Campbell cousins, though sometimes we are negligent in keeping close touch. Faye died when I was a young woman. Billy died some years later.

For a few years, Bobby and his wife, Pat, lived in Wichita Falls. Bill and I visited with them a few times, and vowed to do it more often. We just got too involved with our own families and, sooner than we thought it would happen, they moved back to Amarillo.

The twins had a friend growing up and going to school in Shamrock, who later moved to Iowa Park.. His name was Bobby Johnson.

In the late 1980's, Bill and I took Karlee to one of the Campbell Family reunions, in Shamrock. She had asked me if they would have a "War Dance". I told Bobby what she had said. He told me he had to be full of "Fire Water" before he could dance!!!! And Fire Water was not being served!

During a picture taking session, a group was standing together, the girls and Bobby, with some of their Indian cousins from Martha's side of the family. Alice said, "Wait! We need Maryanne in this one."

I responded, "You don't want any old White girl in your family picture!" As if it was rehearsed, together both Bobby and Alice turned to me and said, "Get up here, PALE EYES!"

We had a wonderful time, and have always intended to go to another. They have also been to the Chambers reunions. The whole family is just great.

Chapter 9

RUPERT AND LILLIAN

Rupert was the grandson of Louis Pearl Chambers, who was also my grandfather. Just as in the case of Matt Campbell, that made him my first cousin. He, too, was the age of my daddy.

I only remember one visit to see Rupert and Lillian. When I was a small child, they lived in Tulsa. I thought that meant they were rich, because everybody knew Tulsa was a big city, and only rich people lived there! We were all very excited about that trip.

To the best of my knowledge, all the children of Rupert and Lillian were grown when we visited them. I only remember adults in the home. And, of course, I couldn't possibly remember which ones they were.

Most of my memories of Rupert and Lillian were created in my teen and early adult years, when the two of them often came to see my Mama and Daddy. In fact, they were visiting in my parents home just east of Iowa Park, when I left for the hospital with my first child. I realize that was rude of me, and I should have waited until after they were gone. However, I was young, and didn't know the proper social behavior..... They were gracious and excused me.

I have always been glad that Bill also met Rupert and Lillian, as I really loved the two of them. Mama and Daddy beamed with happiness while they were there.

In 1994, Barbara Chambers Wolfforth was found as we sent out letters about our Chambers family reunion at the RAC building in Iowa Park. And she came to that one. Barbara is the granddaughter of Rupert and Lillian. Since then, she has attended other reunions, and she and I have stayed in contact through e-mail. We are truly friends.

A few years later, a great-grandson of Rupert and Lillian found us, and came to a reunion with his wife and family. That's how we became attached to Feller and Lisa Chambers.

I have always wanted to know the other descendants of those cousins I loved so much. Maybe someday I will meet more of them.

Chapter 10

AUNT NORA AND UNCLE WOODY

My Mama's sister married Woody Walls a short time after Mama and Daddy were married. Aunt Nora and Uncle Woody lived at Cleburne, Texas. That was a long way from Wynona, Oklahoma, in the 1930's. But our family made at least one trip to see them, and I remember it very well.

The ages of the older children were very close to those of my older siblings. They were all girls. Then, they had two boys. Woody Jr. was just Charlotte's age. Frank was just slightly older than me.

I remember the four of us playing in a haystack. Charlotte crawled up on the top. We had no way of knowing that haystacks often decay on the inside, and leave a hollow hill. Charlotte went through the straw, and landed on the inside of the stack.

Maybe we weren't supposed to be playing on the haystack. That's the only reason I can imagine now that kept us from calling our parents to help save her. But I do remember the two boys and I began digging frantically to get her out. I don't remember how it turned out.... but obviously, I still have my sister! So I guess we succeeded in getting to her before the dust killed her.

All the other times I remember seeing Aunt Nora and Uncle Woody and the boys were at Grandma's house.

During the summer before my senior year in high school, Frank came to visit us a while. I always liked Frank. Anyway, while he was there, we double dated quite a lot. I don't even remember what boy I was with at the time.

After we were grown, we lost touch. I tried to contact him in recent years, to no avail. I just wonder if Frank remembers that summer as fondly as I do.

Woody Jr. and his wife, Laverne, came to our Chambers Family Reunion in 1994, the same year Barbara Wolfforth was there. In more recent years, they haven't been able to come, because Laverne had a stroke. That is just one more of the family contacts that I have neglected. It's time for me to write to them. We are not getting younger!

Chapter 11

WOOSTER MOUND

Yes, there really was a Wooster Mound. I started the third grade at Wooster Mound school.... a two room frame building, set just a short distance from a mound of earth that rose out of flat land. The last time I was there, it had shrunk from my childhood eyes..... But it was still impressive. The school had grades one through four in one room, and grades five through eight in the other. Charlotte was in the other room.

By that time, Nina and Roberta had graduated and gone off to nurse's training in Muskogee. Tommy had just gone into high school the year before, so he still went to school in Wynona.

I have fond memories of Wooster Mound school. There were four children in my grade.... the other girl was Doris Shaw. Then, there was Samuel Orr, and Burl Gene Hawkins. I liked Samuel best, but Burl Gene was in love with me. Every day, he would slip up behind my chair, and kiss me on the cheek.... then run!!!! He finally won my heart.

At lunch, all the kids went out to a separate little house where the mothers cooked for us. Each week, two mothers cooked, with all of them taking turns during the school year.

We had prayer before we ate.... and we all hated carrots! We tried to learn how to get them down without tasting them. There were a lot of methods offered by the older, more experienced kids, but I never accomplished it. Every week, we had carrots for one meal. And we had to eat at least two bites of everything on our plates.

One little boy .... I don't remember his name.... came to our school for one semester. He was not allowed to say the pledge with us, or pray with us, or eat with us. I never knew why. But while the

37

rest of us were eating, we could see him peeking into the window. I remember how lonely he looked. I always wanted him to come in.

My best friend was Betty Jo VanCleve. She was a grade ahead of me. But their farm was the closest neighbor with a girl for me to play with. I spent a lot of time there. Sometimes, I didn't like her, because she had so many dolls, and still got the biggest one at our Christmas party at school. I was jealous of her.

But then, one day, she made her daddy mad, and even though I was visiting, he made her go outside. I saw him take his belt off, and watched through the window as he beat that little girl without mercy. I never envied her again.

I loved our home. Out front, there was a fish pond, with a fountain shooting up from the center. I used to sit on the flagstones that bordered it, watching the fish and dreaming the hours away.

The road out front wasn't very busy, since neighbors were few and far between. But still, Charlotte and I had a lemonade stand. We sat for hours, waiting for a customer. And, sure enough, when a car did come by, it always stopped and the person bought a glass of lemonade. Not only was that the thing to do for little girls, but chances were that they really were thirsty, and Mama made sure out lemonade was good.... and cold.

We always had ice in our refrigerator..... a modern convenience that our friends didn't have. But we envied others for that big block in their ice boxes, where ice could be chipped off at will.

Their wood fires and kerosene lamps fascinated us, too. But the most amazing thing I ever saw was that cream separator on the back porch of the VanCleve's home. You just poured the milk in the top, and without a good reason, the milk came out one spout and the cream came out from another! Living on a farm was far different from living at a gasoline plant.

Daddy was handy with making the most of what he had at hand. At the plant, the engines were cooled by water that circulated through them and back into a huge cooling house, called a 'tower'.

As it came off the engines, it was hot. So, Daddy built a little stall in one of the plant buildings, and made a shower for us, using that water. He also put a real washing machine there for Mama, so that she didn't have to heat the water for her laundry, and certainly didn't have to use the iron wash pots our neighbors used.

The cooling tower was made of tall walls of louvers that the water ran over. As it fell into the tank below, the air flowing through from the outside became cool, too. The walk-ways around it were narrow, and it really was dangerous for little girls to be in there. But, once in a while, on a hot summer day, I would slip inside the door, for a few minutes. I never got caught. More fortunately, I never slipped.

When Bus came to spend time with Tommy, they always seemed to build something that lasted. In the woods at the back of the plant property, they built the best tree house I have ever seen. The ladder up was secure and easy enough for a little girl to climb. And they allowed Charlotte and me to play in it, when they were doing something else.

There is something magical about a real tree house.... high above the world below, where you could see across clearings all the way to the neighbors' houses. I have never forgotten it.

Most of the kids got to ride their horses to school. There was a shed where they were put into stalls during the day, and bales of hay for them to eat. I had a horse.... well, I was allowed to call her mine.... named Strawberry. She loved me, and I could ride her all day long. But as soon as Charlotte got on her, she would head for a tree to run under, and rake her off.

Since Charlotte either had to walk, or be taken in the car to school, I had to go with her most of the time. But the few times I was allowed to ride Strawberry to school, I felt like I belonged to the Horse crowd!!!! The big boys unsaddled her, and saddled her again in the afternoon for me.

I've always loved horses. To this day, the best part of any parade is the horses.... and usually a "Grand Marshall" of the parade is riding up front. Wooster Mound and Wynona were near Pawhuska, the bigger town where we did our weekly shopping and we went to parades there several times. Pawhuska was the home of Bob Wills for many years and, one year, he was the Grand Marshall.

I got as far in the street as possible to get a good look at the most famous man I knew of at that age. But my joy was doubled when he rode down the block, got off his horse, and ambled back up the street with a group of men. I've always wondered why I was the one, with many children lining the street, but as he passed, he reached down and patted my head. If 8 year old children can fall in love, I did at that very moment!

One of my favorite memories is about a car Daddy bought for Tommy. I don't remember if Daddy had to drive him to school, or if the bus came out that far at the time. But he was 16, and that may have been enough reason. It was a beautiful Model A Roadster. To this day, Tommy remembers that car as the joy of his life.

My big brother even allowed Charlotte and me to ride with him sometimes. I loved riding in the rumble seat. Charlotte liked to sit up front with Tommy. One day, we had been out riding around, and had just passed Wooster Mound schoolhouse, and a home that was across the road from it. Tommy looked back at something, and the next thing we knew, we were sitting in the ditch. It scared all of us, but Tommy was really upset.

He told us girls to sit still, while he ran home to get Daddy. When they drove up, Daddy calmly got behind the wheel, and drove the car out of the ditch!!!! Poor Tommy was so embarrassed.... but extremely relieved that he had not damaged the love of his life.... and that Daddy was not mad at him.

After we moved to Wooster Mound, we continued going to church in Wynona, when the folks could go. Daddy was saved there, and poured his whole heart into the church.

We often went to auctions. Usually, they were all livestock. But once, there was a beautiful piano. My teacher at school taught piano after school, and all my friends took lessons from her. I wanted a piano more than anything in the world. I was ecstatic when Daddy was high bidder on that instrument. My joy was short lived. Daddy gave it to the church. I was crushed. That's the only time I remember being really mad at Daddy. I never forgave him.

...life changed forever...

Chapter 12

MY WORLD SHAKEN UP

December 7, 1941, our world came crashing down as Japan attacked the military base in Honolulu, Hawaii. At that time, Hawaii was a United States possession, rather than a state. A Japanese 'diplomat' was in Washington D.C., smiling on our officials, as the attack was preparing to take place. The history books will never tell the truth about the deliberate ploy to distract our government into trusting the Japanese at the time.

We all listened to the radio that Sunday morning as President Franklin Roosevelt announced that we were at war. Life changed forever.

Everybody loved the school at Wooster Mound, and I spent two wonderful years there. But the most traumatic era in our young lives had begun, and with it, Wooster Mound closed. We had to be bussed back to Wynona. So, I began the fifth grade in the same school where I started four years earlier.

But soon after, another move occurred, this one unexpected and just as traumatic to our family as the beginning of the war the previous year.

The winter of 1942-43 was brutal in northern Oklahoma. School let out early when the storm began that January day. Tommy had driven his car to school, and was not with Charlotte and me on the bus.

As the two of us stepped down, the snow was up to our waists, the wind was blowing, and with no telephone, our folks didn't know the schedule had been changed. It was a fourth of a mile to our house, down a little hill to a culvert for water to pass under, then back up the other side.

I was crying, and wanted to crawl into the culvert to get away from the wind, but Charlotte pulled me on, insisting that it was too cold for us to stop. I hated my big sister for bossing me. I probably have never thanked her for saving my life.

When we reached our house, it was freezing cold inside, too. Mama wrapped us in blankets and did her best to warm us, to no avail. She was angry at the bus driver for leaving us alone, and distraught over worry about Tommy getting home. I don't remember how, but he finally made it in.

The gas supply to the plant had been cut off, and Daddy was out walking the lines to find the break. In the process, his hands were frost-bitten, and he was totally exhausted when he came in. I can't remember how long it was before he learned that another company had interrupted the service to our plant, without regard for our very lives.

Since Daddy had already received his transfer to Clara, Texas, our parents made rapid decisions to pack Charlotte and me into the car, leave Tommy with our friends, the Culp family, and start driving south. At least, we would have some heat from the motor, and it was better than staying in the house with no heat at all.

So, without packing anything but what clothes we could carry, and quilts to wrap us, we said goodbye to our brother.... Mama and Daddy said goodbye to their son, knowing full well that he would probably never again live in the home with us..... and we began the long drive to Texas. The war-time speed limit was 45 miles per hour, to conserve gas. Of course, the gas was rationed.....and no one had ever heard of Interstate Highways....

I just imagine that while Mama was heart-broken over leaving her son behind, she was thanking God that none of us had died in the cold.....and even though the trip ahead was going to be hard, at least most of the roads were paved.....and instead of a horse and buggy, we were riding in an enclosed car. I'm sure all the previous journeys in her life came to her mind.

Chapter 13

WORLD WAR II

This is going to be a difficult subject for me to fully cover. That war was not like it is today.... something that happens someplace else.... and you think about it when the subject comes up. The WAR was part of our daily lives, it ruled our thoughts every minute, what we had to wear, what we ate, and how we lived in our homes.... even our behavior.

Nina was married to Tommy Craig by then, but Roberta was a nurse. It seemed like the only thing for her to do was join the Army Nurse Corps. She was 22 years old.

Not long afterward, Tommy was drafted out of his senior year of high school, because he turned 18, and had enough credits to graduate without finishing the year.

The rest of us had already moved to Clara, Texas, when that happened. He had just enough time to come spend a few days with us, and bring Spot home to us, before he headed off to training. The training was brief, because men were needed in the battles.

So, Mama and Daddy had two children in the war. Plus their son-in-law Tommy Craig went into the Navy, leaving Nina at home with little Johnny. She came to Clara, and lived in the empty school house.

In the windows of nearly every home, there hung a small 'flag', with a blue background and gold fringe along the border. It hung from a gold cord with a tassel. On each flag, there was one star for each family member that was in the service. If they were still living, the stars were white. Those that had been killed in the war had gold stars to represent them. Our flag had two white stars. We prayed that they were never changed to gold, as many of our friends homes had.

I don't remember where Tommy Craig served, but both Tommy and Roberta were in Europe. The most gut-wrenching experience I ever had as a child was walking into the house without Mama hearing me, and seeing her sitting at the table, screaming and crying, and praying with all her might for the safety of her children. Over and over, I heard her cry, "He's just a little boy..." Mama's little boy would come back from the war a decorated hero.

At home, each member of the family had a book of food stamps, and another one for clothing and shoes. Without those stamps, we could not buy anything, regardless of how badly we needed it, or how much money we had.

For the automobiles, there were gasoline stamps and tire stamps. When your allotment ran out, you did without. It was a discipline that our society couldn't handle in today's world.

The threat of our country being bombed was ever present. Planes depended on sight for targets. So, before we turned the lights on at night, the windows had to be covered with heavy black cloth that would not allow a glint of light outside.

Before a door was opened to go to the toilet, the lights were turned off, and no flash lights could be used. There was no driving after dark, no street lights, no business signs with lights. We lived under black-out orders.

The war was financed by War Bonds. Everybody bought them. The cheapest one cost $18.75, and would be worth $25 when it matured in 10 years. At school, we saved our money until we had a quarter... then we bought a Savings Bond Stamp. It went into a book. When our book was full with $18.75 worth of stamps, we took it to the Post Office and traded it for a $25 bond.

The war was personal, even to a spoiled 10 year old girl.

Chapter 14

CLARA, TEXAS

That cold winter drive across Oklahoma to our new home finally ended. Clara is about 12 miles north of Iowa Park, and about the same distance west of Burkburnett. The Skelly office was in Burkburnett.

Daddy located the house we were to live in, and Mama exploded! It was a far cry from the nice home we had left. So, Daddy drove back into the office at Burkburnett, and had a conference with headquarters. After promises of getting the house repaired, and painted, Mama finally relented. We stayed in Burkburnett with friends of the folks, until the van with our possessions arrived.

When we first enrolled in the Burkburnett school, I was in the middle of the 5th grade. Just the year before, Texas had gone from an 11 year school schedule to 12 years like other states. They did that by changing the number of each grade to the next one above.

I was in the 5th grade in Oklahoma, because I had gone to school 4 previous years. Then, I was put in 5th grade in Texas. Therefore, I was one year older than the kids in my class, and had already taken everything they were studying at the time. The result was that I was labeled a genius by the teachers that just didn't get it.

The school system should have caught the mistake, and placed me in the class where I belonged. But they didn't, and the age difference was brought up to me all the way through school. The same thing happened to Charlotte.

The two deepest friendships that lasted throughout my life were born with our move to Clara. First, there was Sandy.... her name was Elsie Williams, but to me, she was always Sandy.

The plant on the Ramming Lease was a two-man operation. Mr. Williams was crippled, and would soon have to stop working. But he was still there when we arrived. The Williams family lived at the north end, and we lived at the south end of the plant. And there was a well-worn path between the two homes within days of our moving in.

There were four kids in that family. At the time, Robert was away in the service, too. So, we just knew the girls. Betty Lou was the oldest. Jackie was Charlotte's age.

Sandy was just a few months older than I was. We hit it off instantly. She was a chubby girl with a big laugh, and maturity beyond her years. She became like a mother hen to me.... always guiding me as if she was an adult.

After Mr. Williams left Skelly, they moved into a house in Burkburnett. That became a second home for Charlotte and me. Mrs. Williams was the mother most girls dream about.... just one of the girls... We loved her very much. And we knew we were always welcome in that home.

Mr. Williams was always cross. He was in a lot of pain, but he was also just a natural grouch. When he wanted coffee, he banged his cup on the table, instead of asking for it. He didn't like other kids around, but for some reason, he liked me. So I was not afraid of him. The others were.

Jackie and Sandy spent a lot of time at our house, too. The Clara school had closed, so we were in the Burkburnett school district. Often, one or both of those girls rode home with us on the bus.

Just as Charlotte and I loved Mrs. Williams, Sandy and Jackie loved our Daddy. Sandy was always hanging across his chair, hugging him from behind. Once in a while, she would crawl into his lap... which I also did until I was almost grown.

Daddy was a gentle man. But I didn't understand the full reason for the attachment until Mr. Williams died, after we were in our late teens. When I started to cry, Sandy got mad at me. She said something to the effect that I should have cried while he was alive. But now, they were all free. She was glad he was dead.

The other life-time friendship started when Mama and Daddy's old friends, George and Nellie Leath heard that we had moved back to Clara. George was no longer working for Skelly, and they lived at Valley View, near Iowa Park.

They came to visit us, with their youngest two children. The girl was Frances, and she was my age. The boy was just a little older than Charlotte, and he had a driver's license, so Daddy let him drive the old car that was used to go around the different meter houses on the lease....and the four of us rode all those country roads, until we knew we had to go back.

We had a ball that day. But that boy and I had no idea that our lives would cross again, and become intertwined as adult family friends. His name was Preston.

I grew to love that home at the Skelly plant, out on the Ramming Lease. Just as he had done at the Wooster Mound plant, Daddy built us a shower. Only, this time, he put it in the house, and bought a hot water heater for my mother. No more heating water on the stove for dishes!

There were three bedrooms in that house.... at least, we made a bedroom out of a tiny room off the kitchen. It was MY room, and it was big enough for a cot. But I soon learned that I had rather sleep with Charlotte. She didn't care.

I can't remember how old I was when I became deathly ill at school. I had an extremely high temperature, and couldn't move my head, shoulders or arms. The school superintendent took me home in his car. I couldn't talk to him, and wondered how he knew where I lived, so far from town.

Mama and Daddy were terrified. For several days, if not weeks, Daddy sat beside my bed, as Mama carried out all the doctor's orders. They fed me through a straw, and sometimes I couldn't swallow that, either.

I never knew what the illness was, if my folks were even told. But I was not quarantined, so it could not have been contagious. Later, I learned that it was thought that I had spinal meningitis. Daddy's brother was crippled from that disease, and died before adulthood, so that was their fear.

Also, they had lost one child. No wonder they were scared. But I recovered with no visible damage to my body or brain. [Oh! I can hear it right now! If my kids are reading this.....here's your answer!]

My favorite spot around our home was on top of the two very tall water tanks, located just across the road, right in front of the house. They were connected by a platform between them, where those long, long stairs led. Charlotte and I sat up there for hours, either together, or with friends. Many times, I sat alone, dreaming about my life, looking across the fields to the church at Clara, and all the neighbor's homes.

We were forbidden to slip off into the water, even after I became a good swimmer.... but once in a while, when that Texas summer sun beat down, I was known to disobey my parents.... especially when Sandy was with me.

Later, as a young teen-ager, I would go up there and watch my boyfriend get his horse out of the barn, saddle him, and ride to my house. Sometimes, I went down to meet him, but it was more fun when he climbed those stairs, and sat on the steps with me.

Chapter 15

BAPTISM

When I was a very small child, my Daddy was saved. For several years following his conversion, our family attended church on a regular basis. I remember lying on a pew before I was old enough to know what was going on. I have flashes of memories of Bible drills. And all of my childhood, and through my teens, Mama and Daddy discussed Scripture, and Christianity. But I do not remember going to Sunday School. I know I did. I just do not remember it.

Then, there was a period after Daddy took over the plant at Wooster Mound that we didn't go to church often. Daddy thought he couldn't be away from the plant, because he was responsible, 24 hours a day. Mama had never driven very much, and she didn't like to drive the distance into Wynona.

After moving to Clara, we didn't immediately join a church. So there were a few years that I was not educated in a church setting, where it would be clear to me what was being said from a pulpit. Five years is a very short time in the life of an adult. It's an eternity in the life of a child.

Easter Sunday, 1944, Mama took Charlotte and me to the First Baptist Church in Burkburnett. That day, the preacher was talking in the Intermediate Department of Sunday School. He was a big pompous man, who had no idea of how to deal with children. The invitation was given, but I had no concept of what it meant.

As far as I was concerned, I had always believed in Jesus, and there was no doubt that I lived in a Christian home. So it was very confusing to me when that man embarrassed me, by walking down the aisle to where I was standing, asking me if I wanted to go to Heaven. Well, of course, I wanted to go to Heaven. Did he think I would say No?

Then, he took my hand and led me to the front of the room, and told the other kids that I had 'accepted Christ'. My friends from school began filing past me, shaking my hand.

I don't remember how I got from there to the sanctuary for the Worship Service. When I found Mama, she was crying. Somebody had told her that her little girl had been saved. Then that damned man did it again, and had me come to the front of the church, just like he had stood me in front of the kids.

Somehow, during the day, somebody decided that Charlotte needed to be saved, too! By that night, it had been arranged for us both to be Baptized....

That experience robbed me of a genuine Baptism after coming face to face with Jesus, as my Savior. I have never forgiven that man. Mama just didn't realize what was happening. After all, I was 12, and in her mind, I had been trained up in the way I should go....

We didn't attend that church very long before we moved outside of town to the Fairview Baptist Church. That's where my Christian training really began.

After Bill and I were married, we were baptized together, trying to make up for the lack of understanding we both felt as children. But it just wasn't the same, because by then, I had been a true Christian for many years.

I pledged to myself that I would not allow that to happen to my own children.

Chapter 16

END OF THE WAR

Two major events took place in 1945. The first was the death of our president, Franklin D. Roosevelt on April 12th. As the news came across the radio, I ran down to the cattle-guard that was the 'gate' to the lease property. Daddy was there, repairing the pipes. When I gave him the news, he fell to the ground and cried out loud. I had never even seen a tear in his eyes.

I cried, too. All my life, except the first year, that man had been our president. All I knew was that my parents worshiped him next to God. And, what would happen to our country?

Harry S Truman became the next president, and history has shown that he was indeed a good one. Nobody knows how much this had to do with what happened next.... But on April 30th, Hitler committed suicide, rather than be captured by our army.....the army where both my brother and sister were serving.

A few months later, on September 2, 1945, the war officially ended, with the surrender of Japan.

All the service men and women came home.....There were celebrations all across the country. No, we didn't watch it on television. We heard it on the radio, saw pictures in the newspapers, and when we went to the movies, we saw the Newsreels, which had kept us familiar with the events all during the war.

Roberta came home with the husband she had married in Germany, Bob Llovet. Then they moved on to New York City, where he was raised.

Tommy was back home with us, for all too short a time. He was the best brother that any girl could ever ask for. He was also the most handsome young man I had ever seen. He taught me to dance, and told me to remove the wart from my ankle, because "glamour girls don't have warts!" [I did!]

When he went to town at night, he always took Charlotte and me with him, and left us at the Williams' until he was ready to go home. Sometimes, we went to the movies. Other times, we would just lie on the lawn and watch for falling stars, and talk about boys.

I often think of how many nights we would have sat home alone, if he had not been so good to us.

Chapter 17

PUPPY LOVE?

My first boyfriend…. [that is, not counting the little boys in 3rd grade] was Jesse Butler. The Butlers and the Dorlands lived near the little store a few miles west of Clara. They all rode our school bus, and were picked up before we were. Jesse always saved a seat for me. I was in the 7th grade then.

Charlotte sometimes dated Robert Dorland A few times, the two of us were with a carload of Dorlands and Butlers. Both had sisters, and Jesse had a brother, Donald. Cars could hold 8 people back then and we packed every inch. So, although I wasn't really old enough to date, I got to go to movies with Jesse. We always drove to Electra, but I've never really known why.

One night, Billy Dorland had the chore of going to the ticket window to ask what was showing that night. The girl in the booth told him, "Too Young To Know". When he came back to the car, he didn't say anything. His face was red. Robert asked him what the movie was. He said, "She wouldn't tell me." After some prodding, he said, "Well, she told me I was too young to know!!!!"

Jesse was my boyfriend all through Junior High. I liked him a lot, but Mama tried hard to convince me that he was not from the "right" family. I didn't know anything about the family, except that they were poor. If Mama knew anything else, she never told me. As I was getting old enough to really date, she often told me I could go with anybody else, but not Jesse. And I would tell her I didn't want to go with anybody except Jesse.

The stand-off was never put to the test, since by the time I could go with a boy anywhere alone, things took another turn.

We went to church at a small place called Fairview, just west of Burkburnett. There, we formed deep friendships with people we would always love, and who crossed our paths from time to time in later years. The most important of those were the Pembertons and the Rogers.

The Rogers lived next to the church. There were three girls... Naomi, Monette, and Wanda and one boy, Murle. Wanda was my age, and Monette was just a little younger than Charlotte. Murle was a little older.

The Pembertons were also our neighbors, who lived just across the highway from the Clara Lutheran Church, and the empty school building. The family consisted of 11 boys and 4 girls. Of course, most of them were married, or living elsewhere as adults. Four of the boys were in the service.

Billy and Donald were the only ones living at home, until the war was over. Then Hubert, Buck and Jay Wilson came home for a while, before moving elsewhere. The others were grown and married. But Billy Jerald was about Charlotte's age, and Donald Ray was in my class.

Lurlene was the oldest Pemberton girl, and was married to Glen Lynskey. They lived nearby, and had two little girls, Janette and Lora Jean. Janette was only a couple of years younger than me, and we became close as time passed.

Both families were among those we met with regularly for old fashioned Stamps music 'singings', usually at the Pemberton's home. There was every possible stringed instrument there, and those boys all played each one of them.

Charlotte became engaged to Murle Rogers. He had dedicated his life to be a minister, and we all loved him. What happened to cause them to break up has never been clear to me. But she carried that pain for many years.

Tommy went to the University of Oklahoma, where he met Marguerite. They were married, and moved to Burkburnett for a while, before Tommy was transferred to Velma, Oklahoma, with Skelly Oil Company.

Charlotte had been the school photographer, and Daddy had set up a dark room in a closet for her, where she developed and printed the pictures she had taken. Her dream was to be a professional photographer.

When she graduated, she moved to Dallas, to live on her own, while working at whatever job she could get. I think the main reason was to get away from seeing Murle with a new girlfriend.

I fell in love with Donald Pemberton. I had seen him every day at school since the 5th grade and every Sunday at church. But when I was 14, there was a church hay ride to Perkins Reservation, with games when we arrived. In one of the games, he chose me to be his partner. On the ride home, we sat together, looking at each other in the moonlight. It could not have been more perfect, or any more real if I had been an adult. From then on, it was Donald and me.

It wasn't easy to tell Jesse that I had a new boyfriend. As young as we were, I can still see the hurt in his eyes. But I couldn't have helped the situation, because I truly had fallen in love for the first time.

Throughout my life, those families…. the Butlers, the Dorlands, the Rogers and the Pembertons have reappeared in various ways. Donald was a part of my life for many years, off and on, up until I got married.

Naomi Rogers married a man named W.A. McClure..... In later years, we learned that W.A. had a cousin named Bill Glasgow.

Monette married Jay Wilson, and would much later become the Wichita County Tax Collector. Bill and I remained friends with them, until both died.

Wanda married a nice guy, and Bill and I used to visit with them when our older boys were just babies. We just lost touch, and I forgot his name.

Murle did become a Baptist minister. Billy Dorland married Mildred Butler. Donald Butler dated Janette Lynskey for a while.

I read about Jesse in the Wichita Falls paper many, many years later. His son-in-law was quoted as saying Jesse was the best man in the world. He was so sweet as a boy that I had no doubt he was a good man.

Janette Lynskey and I remained close friends for many, many years. She was again to become part of my life, when we were adults.

I went to school at Burk for five years, which was longer than any other. I was in the high school band there, and played basketball. I had lots of friends, besides my boyfriend, Donald.

I hated to move, but Daddy was retiring from Skelly. He had bought an acreage at Iowa Park. My sophomore year would begin there.

Chapter 18

IOWA PARK

Sometimes life changes completely in a very short period of time. Any move from one locality to another is a new phase. But the move to Iowa Park brought about so many new things to my life and that of my parents that it was hard to absorb it all.

It was the first home that Mama and Daddy had ever owned. The ten acres was just outside the Iowa Park city limits on a four lane divided highway, which was the first of such roads anywhere around.

There was no plant with its constant rhythmic sound of "pump-pump- pump-pump" that assured us that the engines were all running. There was in its place an eerie silence....the first time in my entire life that I had not gone to sleep by the noise of the plant.

Across the highway was the railroad track. In the middle of the night, if we had finally drifted off, we were brought up out of our beds by the whistle of a freight train as it approached town. It took months to adjust to the change.

The house itself was a castle beside all those we had lived in before. Basically, it was built in the same shape, with the living room, dining room and kitchen all in a straight line, and the two bedrooms on one side. But this one had a little hall leading to the bedrooms, and in the middle of it was a real bathroom. Not just a shower, but a commode, tub and basin. That was the first time we had a bathroom in the house.

The biggest change of all was that I was now an only child. I had a real room all to myself. And while all the repairs were being made to our new home, I was allowed to pick my wallpaper.

I chose a beautiful pattern of pink and yellow roses, running through blue ribbons on a white background. I had my own closet, and my own chest of drawers and dresser.... and a full size bed.

In the dining room, there hung a telephone on the wall. There was no dial. You just picked it up and cranked the handle. The operator came on the line, and asked you who you wanted to talk to. Then she rang it. If she wanted to, she could listen as you talked.

By then, the Pembertons also had a telephone. Donald and I kept it busy, until the folks on both ends got the long distance bills. After that, our calls were limited. He couldn't get the pickup very often, even though he had a license at 15, as farm boys did back then. It was a big family with others wanting to go places, too.

So, we were as separated by 12 miles as we would have been by 12 states. No matter how nice a home we had, I hated it, because I was away from all my friends, and my boyfriend especially.

When I entered the building to enroll at W.F. George High School in Iowa Park that September of 1947, the halls were empty. Only new students had to register that day, and that year, I was the only one.

As I walked into the office, a huge man in overalls passed by me, smiled and said "Good Morning!" Then he pointed to the desk where a young woman sat. She took my name and records from Burkburnett, and told me she was glad I was there. I asked who the man was, and she said, "He is the superintendent."

The young woman's name was Lorene Battles and the man in overalls was W.R. Bradford.

All the other students had been assigned to their rooms the previous spring. I didn't choose to take home-economics, as girls were expected to do. So, I was placed in a home room full of BOYS.

At least, the teacher was a female.... but she and I didn't like each other, so I was pretty alone. The truth can now be told.... she was mad, because she had thought she was going to be in that room with all those boys, all by herself. There has always been one in every school, and she was the teacher with an eye for males of any age, as we all learned with time.

It took a while before I was accepted by the entire group. Most of them resented having to consider that a girl was among them. That teacher didn't count. She had a dirtier mouth than any of them.

One morning, I was among those who had arrived and were seated when a couple of boys entered the door, laughing loud, and one of them cursing. There was a quiet boy seated at the front, on the row by the door. He said, "Watch it, Gilmore! There's a lady in here."The offender looked across the room, straight at me. "Where's a lady?" he said. "I don't see any lady!"

I was embarrassed and angry. The boy who had first spoken raised up in his seat, ready for battle. The teacher stepped in, and said something to the effect of "Cool it!" That was my introduction to Billy Joe Gilmore and Leonard Whisenhunt.

Once a week, in this new school, everybody went to the auditorium for what was called "assembly". It began with prayer, and the pledge of allegiance. It was an informal time when Mr. Bradford spoke to all the students, discussing plans and expectations. And, he introduced new students... in this case, ME....

He asked me to stand. I was uncomfortable with the whole school turned looking at me. He told them my name, and said "When Maryanne enrolled, she looked at me in my overalls and thought I was the janitor!"

The room roared in laughter. My face turned red, and I sat down. But I had no problem being recognized from that day on. The kids all smiled at me in the halls, and I made friends rapidly.

I loved assembly after that. We had other new kids move in, and they got the same type of introduction, to make them feel welcome. And, during each session, we sang Mr. Bradford's favorite song. The name of it was "I LOVE LIFE". And he did! I still remember most of the words, if not all. It went like this:

I love life, and I want to live.
Drink of life's fullness
Take all it can give.
I love life! Every moment must count
To glory in it's splendor,
To revel in it's fount.
I love life! I want to live!

I LOVE LIFE!

The words were emphasized by both the music teacher, Maudie Owens, and Mr. Bradford hitting the air with their fists with each beat. At the end of the song, everybody cheered, and we left the auditorium happy, and ready to get on with the day.

How wonderful it would be if schools could be like that now. Yes, there were problems. And Mr. Bradford was a harsh disciplinarian. He would not have survived in today's world. But he loved every kid in that school, and knew them by name. There was a principal, but he was just there. Mr. Bradford ran everything in person.

My immediate circle of friends at school began with Katy Merle Sumrall. We hit it off in the very beginning, though both of us branched out into other friendships, we remained best of friends.

We had only been at Iowa Park a few weeks when Daddy had a severe attack, similar to epilepsy. He turned ash gray, and his eyes rolled back into his head.   I had driven the car out on the lease, but never on main roads. But I had no choice. I got in the car and drove to Dr. Gordon Clark's house. I was terrified that my Daddy was dying.

Grandma had broken her leg, and was living with us at the time. When I got back to the house, ahead of Dr. Clark, Grandma had gotten a bottle of whiskey out of her suitcase [a gift, of course...]

and poured it straight down Daddy's throat. Dr. Clark said she saved his life.

From that time on, Grandma wouldn't use the wheel chair to move around in. She would walk on her cast, pushing the chair, then sit in it!!! That was my Grandma!!! I loved having her there, even though it meant giving up my room. I would have kept her forever, if she would have stayed.

As soon as he recovered fully, Daddy took me to the Highway Patrol office, and filled out papers for me to get my driver's license, under a hardship clause. He told me that if I was responsible enough to go get the doctor, then I was responsible enough for him to let me drive, and I took full advantage of that!

I loved school. I had the reputation as the smartest girl around. And I have to confess, it was TRUE! Some of the kids called me 'Einstein', but I didn't care about anything but the fun part. I didn't have to study, but then I wasn't trying to get a scholarship, which would have been the smart thing to do.

Today, we have a group of friends that meet regularly, which we fondly call 'Old Friends'. Most of those kids I met that first year are now a part of that group. We weren't all as close in school as we have grown over the years since, but they have become a very important part of my life.

Maudie Owens discovered that I had a good voice and put me in a trio with Betty Perry and Paula Ralston. For two school years, we sang at every social function that arose, as well as being invited to sing at every church in town.

I enjoyed performing in public. But Mama thrived on my fame! She spent a lot of time sewing up new clothes for me to wear for those events.   She had great dreams for me.

Mama was very happy in her own home. Her kitchen was a galley style, very easy for her work in. I would come home from school and find her with the radio on, singing along. Often, when I stepped in the door, she would grab me, and dance me around the room.

Sometimes, if Daddy was going to be outside for a while, I would get my make-up, and 'paint' her face, as she called it. She loved to wear lipstick, but Daddy didn't approve. So, as soon as the screen door of the back porch slammed, she would run to the bathroom, and wash her face. We both enjoyed that game and we never got caught!

Chapter 19

LOVE AND INFATUATION

Leonard was my hero. He looked after me while I got acquainted in those new surroundings. I still loved Donald Ray, but I was 15, and like all teen-aged kids, I needed to be a part of what was going on in my school. Leonard became my escort. He knew I had a boyfriend at Burkburnett, but he had his own plans.

Later, he told me that he had seen me on the stairs that first day of school, and fell in love immediately. Who cares if it was true? It was romantic! And it would explain his anger at Bill for insulting me. I believed him.

Donald Ray came over when he could, mostly on Sunday afternoons, when his parents came to visit with Mama and Daddy, too. Real dates were few and far between. He didn't want me to date anybody else, and it caused a lot of problems between us.

It all came to a head one night when Katy Merle had a party at her house. Leonard took me. I had no idea that Donald would come over that night. Mama told him where I was. He knew where Katy lived, because he had been there previously with me. So, he went to her house, without knowing that I was with Leonard.

Mama thought that by sending Donald to the party, I would dump Leonard. She wanted me to continue dating just Donald, and eventually marry him. But the ploy back-fired. As I walked outside with him, Leonard followed us to the pickup. The two boys shook hands, as Donald said, "Take good care of her." Leonard assured him that he would.... and Donald drove off.

That was not the way I wanted it to end. In fact, I didn't want it to end at all, and couldn't understand why I couldn't just keep them both. I really was growing more and more attached to Leonard, but I didn't want to let go of Donald. I think most young girls go through that. I just wonder if it hurts them all as much as it did me.

There were still occasional visits between our homes, and we talked on the telephone once in a while, but Donald began dating other girls, and told me I couldn't be his girlfriend anymore.

I honestly don't know of any particular point when I can say that I fell in love with Leonard. As the months went by, I just knew I loved him. When he asked me if I would marry him, it was natural for me to say yes. He bought a beautiful set of rings, and I wore the engagement ring from then on, through our junior year.

We were together constantly, either at his house, or mine, or out on a double date with Bobby Bohannan, and any one of a variety of girls. Saturday nights, we went to Youth Night at the Church of God. On Sundays, we went to First Baptist Church. That's where he was saved.

When we were at the Whisenhunt's home, they often had a family of friends there by the name of Forsan. There was a beautiful girl in that family, just our age. Her name was Nettie. She and her siblings went to school at Valley View. I briefly wondered why Leonard fell for me, when Nettie was there in his home so often. But I didn't worry about it.... much.

It was during this time that I had my first job. It only lasted a few months, because of the transportation problem of living in Iowa Park and working in Wichita Falls. Riding the bus on a regular basis was expensive, even though it stopped out on the highway to pick me up, and drop me off.

Back then, there were 'dime stores' in every town, and that's where teen-aged girls would usually work. Some of them were Woolworths, Kresses, and Ben Franklins. I went to work at McCroy's on Indiana Street, after school and on Saturdays.

There was another girl from Iowa Park who worked there, as well as her mother, Mrs. Boyd. The girl was Iona. We became friends, even though she had graduated from high school before I moved to Iowa Park. We would sit and talk about boyfriends during our lunch break. I had never met him, but I felt like I knew Bud Patterson very well....

In later years, we would cross paths many times. After we both married, we were in the same Sunday School class. Then, she became a Pentecostal, and tried very hard to get me to leave the Baptist Church. But we still loved each other. We became neighbors, and the little Patterson boys grew up with mine.

Leonard and I fought a lot. I don't remember why, except that he loved cars, and when he got a new one, he liked it better than he did me! Or so I thought. But we had a lot of fun, too.

I'm not sure why I wanted to end the relationship, but it didn't happen with a fight, or jealousy. All I remember is, Leonard walked me to the door. I took off my ring and gave it back to him, telling him, "I don't love you the way I should."

We didn't see each other after that. He quit school, telling Bobby that he just couldn't face seeing me every day. Bobby kept him informed of everything I did, and in turn, told me when Leonard said something about me. For a while, I thought he would probably try to get me back. But he didn't.

For more than half a century after that, we crossed paths without seeing each other, or even knowing it. Leonard married Nettie soon after Bill and I married. They lived near Nina, in Oklahoma City, and I passed their house within yelling distance. They also visited her sister, Bernice Todd, just a few blocks from our home, in Iowa Park. Also, the Todd's son, Gerald, and our Billy were very close friends in school

Neither of us had any idea that we would become family friends in our old age.

I dated several different guys after Leonard and I broke up, in the few months before my senior year, and a few weeks into that school year. Among them was a boy named Billy Spruiell. We didn't really hit it off.

Another was Jug Davis. I made the mistake of beating him in a swimming race across the length of the deep end of Sand Beach. That ended that.

I really liked Patsy Steed's brother, Benny. He was separated from his wife, and both my parents and his approved of our dating, but he and his wife reconciled.

It certainly wasn't a date, but one day, a jeep pulled into our drive. I went out to see who it was. Behind the wheel was that boy, Billy Joe Gilmore. The other kid was Tunk Taylor. I never knew why they came to see me... probably, they were just driving down the highway, and my house was handy, and they decided to show off.

Anyway, they told me the jeep belonged to the National Guard..... and so did Bill.... No doubt, it was not supposed to be out on the roads for fun. But Bill asked me if I wanted to ride to town with them. I said, "Sure!"

I expected to be seated in the front passenger seat, like a lady. But, NO! They stuck me on the back seat like a trophy and took off. I was conspicuous, and uncomfortable... and not very happy.... They couldn't get me home soon enough!

Then.... there was that soldier, home on leave. His name was Paul Gilstrap. He had graduated from Iowa Park before I moved there.

We met downtown, in front of the drugstore. All the girls with me knew him, and told me he was okay. We made a date for the next night.... and the next.... and the next. We were together every night until his leave was up. Sometimes, we were with other kids.

When he had to go to the bus station to go back to camp, his friends Choice Brown and Alton Hunter, and their girlfriends took him. Of course, they took me along, too, and brought me back home.

I liked him, and we had a really good time while he was home, but I dismissed it as just another date.

Soon, the most beautiful love letters began to arrive, almost daily. I oohed and aahed over them, and showed them to all the girls. And they oohed and aahed over them.....

Such poetry! Such glowing words about me! I wrote back, but said nothing even faintly similar to Paul's letters.

*...kids hanging out the windows
and maybe even one or two on the hood...*

Chapter 20

FUN AND GAMES

A few weeks later, the Texas-Oklahoma Fair started, as always, at the fairgrounds where the shopping center and old Walmart store stands today, across the block from our home in Iowa Park.

We had our senior booth where parents cooked, and we served the crowds. One shift, I was assigned to wash dishes with Billy Joe Gilmore. Sparks flew when I handed him a dish to dry..... I completely forgot that this was the guy who had insulted me a couple of years before.... and later had actually hit me in the eye with a paper wad in study hall. In fact, I wasn't even sure he was the same guy, at all.

Maudie Owens was also working in the booth, that shift. She saw the way that Bill and I were looking at each other. She came up behind us, putting an arm around each of us, and said.

"Kids, you are entering a wonderful time of life. You have plenty of time. Just don't rush it!"

We both brushed it off. But we have remembered that the precious woman was aware of things that we had not even dreamed.

Daddy had given me a car just before school started. It was a Model B Ford. He gave me strict orders that I was not to allow anybody else to drive it. I was one of about 5 kids that had a car at school. It was quite a status symbol, regardless of its age.... or maybe, because of it.

From the school house to the fair, I carried as many kids as could be seated in it. But, from the fair, back to town, it was another story!

First of all, that guy, Billy Joe Gilmore wanted to drive my car.... I let him.....and everybody in sight wanted to climb on. I let them..... We drove down the boulevard with kids on the back end, kids on the running boards, kids hanging out the windows, and maybe even one or two on the hood.

71

Billy Joe won a cute little monkey at one of the carnival shows. He hung it on my rear-view mirror. It hung there until a guy by the name of Billy Dean James reached in the window and swiped it. Later, Billy Joe accused me of giving it away, but I loved that little monkey.

I have no idea how my Daddy heard about the escapade through town.... just because I was the only kid with a car like that.... and just because the boy doing the 'driving' scraped another vehicle.... And my Daddy was just mean enough to take my car away from me, for no reason at all!!!!

After that little episode, I waited patiently for the guy to ask me for a date. It never happened!

Katy Merle also was wanting to date a boy named Gene Regan, so she and I decided we would do the asking. First, we needed money. So, we hired out in the cotton patch, and pulled bolls one whole day. Our hands were so torn up, we had to hide them. But we had the money. Then, I had to borrow Daddy's car, since I had lost my own. It was no easy task, but I got it.

Mrs. Sumrall was absolutely adamant that nice girls didn't ask boys for dates. Katy didn't always stand up to her, but that time, she did. My mama thought it was funny, and both daddies just grinned.

The boys both accepted. So, we put 5 gallons of gas in Daddy's car. That took a whole dollar, at 20 cent a gallon. It cost us another dollar to get into the Shepard Drive In on the old Iowa Park highway. We wined and dined the boys on all the popcorn, cokes and candy we could all hold. It was really a romantic evening!

So, that's how it started. Katy and Gene fell madly in love. And Billy Joe fell madly in love. Me? Oh, he just kind of grew on me.

I was still writing to Paul. He knew I was dating, and never expected me not to. His letters were still very intense. And I still thought it was just a game with him. In fact, Billy Joe helped me when I baked cookies to send to him.

It was a fun time. Most of the time, I borrowed Daddy's car, but when I couldn't get it, Bill would borrow one from his friend, George Speed, known as Speedy.

Speedy worked at the ice house, after returning home from the Navy in WWII. He was older, handsome, and all my girlfriends went wild over him. He and Billy Joe and James Hair were very good friends.

Eventually, Speedy sold that old 1937 Ford to Bill, and his brother, Bud, whom I had not yet met.

We double dated a lot, too. The other couple was usually either Katy and Gene, or James Hair and Wanda Dillard.

By Christmas, Bill and I had decided we wanted to get married. It was something we had not done before!   He bought a wedding band, and we planned to elope secretly on New Years Eve.

Neither of us thought about the fact that we were not of legal age. But, anyway, each of us had such a nice Christmas with our folks that we decided to wait a while.

...the end of my childhood...

Chapter 21

FACING ADULTHOOD

Another six weeks was all Billy Joe and I could wait. Giggles [LaVerne Walters] and Bill Harrington had gotten married a few days before, and we couldn't stand for them to get ahead of us!

By then, I had turned 18, and didn't need permission. Bill talked his Mama into signing for him, telling her if she didn't, we would run away.

So, we went for the mandatory blood test before getting a license. James and Wanda went with us. We all skipped school that day. Then we got the license, and drove to Henrietta to the Justice of the Peace, Doc Worsham the following Sunday. His mama went with us.

I can hear him now....."D-o-o-o- Y-o-o-u B-u-l-l-l-y J-o-o-e take M-u-r-r-y-a-a-n-n-e..............

We still had $5 left after the ceremony, so we went to a drive-in for lunch. The food cost $4, so we tipped the car hop our last dollar, before driving back to Iowa Park.

He took his Mama home. Then we wasted a few more day-light hours, until we could go parking a while, before he took me home. It was a beautiful wedding.......

The following morning, Monday, we went to school and were swarmed by all our friends yelling "Congratulations!!!!" It seemed that we hadn't asked questions about the girl who gave our blood tests. She went to church at Pleasant Valley with a lot of our friends. Of course, knowing we were from Iowa Park, she had to tell them......

So, we went down to the office, to face Mr. Bradford. He told us we could stay in school. But he expelled Wanda and James for skipping school on Friday!

Then, we went home to tell Mama and Daddy before they heard it from somebody else. It was the hardest thing I ever had to do.

They were so hurt that it spoiled all the happiness that the two of us felt.

And in a few days, Billy Joe's brother, Buddy, came home unexpectedly from the Navy, thinking the two of them were going to have great times. He was crushed.

His sister, Veneta made her first big mistake with me, when she swatted me on the butt, as if she was in authority. I refrained from swatting her across the face. It took us a few years to become good friends, but once she accepted the fact that Billy Joe was not her little boy, we got along fine.

His daddy loved me from day one. I became his favorite dance partner around the house and he was a very smooth dancer.

I also had to write to Paul, and tell him I was married. I guess I expected him to be happy, and keep writing to me.... I never heard from him again.

A few years later, Veneta answered her door to a college student who was paying his way by selling something door to door.... and she recognized Paul Gilstrap. She visited with him, full of enthusiasm, talking about her brother, Billy Joe, and his wife......

Finally, as she told me later, Paul interrupted her with, "Well, you DO know that your brother stole my girlfriend, don't you?" She was completely unaware that I had dated Paul, or even knew him.

The next time she saw me, she erupted like a volcano..."WHY DIDN'T YOU TELL ME ABOUT PAUL?????" When I regained my senses, I responded that there was nothing to tell. I had no idea that Paul was serious.

I spent the next 45 years feeling guilty about hurting Paul. Then, at our alumni banquet, his class was celebrating their 50th reunion. When I heard his name, I searched the room, and located him.

After the banquet was over, I maneuvered over to his table before he disappeared. As I introduced myself to the distinguished looking man, he hugged and kissed me, as he very suavely asked, "Who??? My dear, the kiss is NOT familiar!!!!!!"

No more guilt for me! I never knew if he really had forgotten me, or if it was pay-back time. Either way, he got me good!!!!

Looking back, Bill and I were never sorry that we got married. We were just sorry for the way we did it. We never had a real wedding. We just got married.

In later years, a friend gushed, "Oh, I remember when you kids got married! I thought you were SO CUTE!" I replied, "Yeah. So did WE!"

Since we wanted to finish school, it was decided that we would live with each set of parents for equal amounts of time. It proved to be difficult, to say the least. But we made it and our parents survived, too!

Bill began working for the pipeline company that was laying the water line from the new Lake Iowa Park to the city, on weekends and after school. And we graduated together.

The End of my Childhood had officially arrived.

End of Book I

BOOK II

Table of Contents
Book II

The Fifties

...the life I was to live...

Chapter 1

TRANSITION

The life I was to live began to take shape even before Bill and I graduated from High School as a married couple. I was pregnant, which established that I was indeed a woman, but I still felt like a teen-ager.

Living with each set of parents had been our first trial. With Mama and Daddy, we had my room, and relative privacy. Daddy was a jewel, even though he was disappointed. He accepted Bill, and tried to make it easier on us.

Mama was another story. I still don't blame her for her anger, but it dominated every minute of every day. She had always possessed the ability to shrink a child with a stern look, and cold eyes. But there was also a warm, loving side, with a beautiful smile, when those same eyes laughed, and seemed to dance. I lost that Mama when I got married. All I had left was the disapproving mother, who did not like my husband, and made no effort to hide it. Poor Bill. Poor ME..... It was all our fault, and we paid dearly.

At the Gilmore's, I was accepted, and loved. There was laughter and forgiveness. But my Pop, as he became known, Jim Gilmore was not a man to respect privacy, even mine. He resented a locked door, because it was his house. Even though we had the only private bedroom in the house, I hardly had time to dress with the door closed.

After school was out, one of our teachers, Mrs. Ralston, offered us her house for the summer, with NO RENT. Her husband had died during the school year. She was going to Denton, to get another degree. Her oldest daughter, Paula, our classmate and friend, would be in the same college with her. The other kids in the family would be put into summer schools there. She wanted somebody in the house, and trusted us to take care of it.

It didn't take but 5 seconds for Bill and me to accept her generous offer. He had gone to work full time for the pipeline company, so money was coming in, but this was a great help.

We have always remembered that as our first home. It was a large, two story house, but we never went upstairs. We had plenty of room.... a living room, dining room, kitchen, bedroom and bath downstairs! I could have lived there forever.

Summer ended, and the Ralston family was returning home. So, we had to find a place to live. Another classmate friend, Laverne Talley had also married during school (it didn't last, and I don't remember the boy's name). We all decided to rent a two bedroom apartment in Wichita Falls together. It was on Bell Street, the next little street just east of Monroe Shopping Center.

Soon after moving in, the pipeline job in Iowa Park was over, and the company was moving on. Several of the boys from school decided to go with them to the next place, which was at Bowie. Bill went, too, leaving me with Laverne and her husband.

As soon as the job in Bowie was done, another move was to be to Healdton, Oklahoma. I just didn't like living apart from Bill, even though we had paid our part of the rent to the apartment. So, I left my things there with Laverne, with the intention of living there when we returned from Healdton. It didn't occur to me that there would always be another job, someplace else....

When it was apparent that we would not be returning to Wichita Falls, and our rent was due, we went back to get our things. We didn't know that Laverne and her husband had moved out a few days before. The landlady had locked us out, and stolen all our possessions.

We went to the sheriff. He was going to go and retrieve our property, until he heard who the woman was. Then he tucked his tail between his legs and said, "That woman is crazy. I'm not going to her house!"

So, we lost all the things that had been given to us in a wedding shower the church had held for us. The most painful of all was a hand-made quilt that Mrs. Pemberton had given us. But there were a lot of things we really needed, as well.

That was only our first experience of many in losing our worldly possessions.

...one big boarding house...

Chapter 2

HEALDTON, OKLAHOMA

Western Pipe Coating was to be Bill's employer for many years ahead, but we didn't know that when I joined him at Healdton.

I had briefly met the man in charge of the job in Iowa Park, while they were living in a trailer park there. That was back when they were called 'trailers', and they were truly Mobile Homes. Nearly all pipeline people lived in trailers, at least part of the time.

I learned the boss was named Herschel Carey. His brother, Cecil, and their brother-in-law Peewee Vaughan owned the company. None of their wives were with them on the job at Healdton, so I didn't meet them until later. But I did see a big, beautiful Cadillac pull up one day, with a woman, and a little boy about 10 years old. I heard that they were Peewee's wife and son. I was impressed with how rich they were. That was my first glimpse of Ruth and little Dennis. The car drove away. They had just come for a visit.

At Healdton, all the employees lived in one big boarding house. There were all those boys from Iowa Park.... Jimmy Arnold, James Hair, Donald Henson, Willis Skinner.... others that I don't remember..... and Bill and me.

The owners of the boarding house were an older couple that also lived there. The woman adopted me, taking care of me as if I was her own teen-aged pregnant daughter. When I was sick, she would come to our room to see about me.

In the dining room there was a huge 'lazy-susan' table, about 10 feet across. At meal time, it was set with all the food in the center to turn as people filled their plates. It was so good that just about the whole town ate there. Everybody sat in the 'Parlor' until a place was vacant at the table. Then the next one in line would take the seat. We never knew who we would be beside, and seldom did we sit beside each other. It was fun, too.

In the evenings, we all sat together in that parlor, visiting until we were ready to go to our rooms. There was one young boy that fell in love with me. He would jump up and run if I asked Bill to get something for me. It became a joke among the 'big boys.'

One evening, I was craving fresh peaches. The boy disappeared for a while. In an hour or so, he came back... and sure enough, he had found some peaches for me! I was so pleased, I could have kissed him. But I was too young to be able to express appreciation with affection. It would have cost that boy dearly.

Over the next ten years, Bill and I would move so many times that I would lose count, and forget a lot of the towns, much less the places we lived. But Healdton left an indelible memory for both of us, and we hated to leave.

Chapter 3

SPOT

Spot was not just a dog. He had been a member of our family for as long as I could remember. Although he was actually Tommy's dog, he belonged to all of us, and we all loved him.

I'm not sure exactly what breed he was, but we called him a Shepard-Collie. I think now that he was more of a cow dog. He was beautiful, and very intelligent. When it was time to milk, Daddy would tell Spot to go get the cows. And there he would go, flying across the pasture, rounding them up. His favorite game was to grab a cow's tail, and hang on as the cow ran for home.

He was a sensitive dog. If I was sad as a child, he knew it. When I cried, I went outside and sat on the step. Spot always came to me, and put his head in my lap, and just looked into my eyes. He didn't demand petting. He just petted me.

As a very pregnant 'grown-up', I spent some time with Daddy at home, in between the job at Healdton, and the next move. Bill was moving equipment. Mama was at Grandma's house.

Spot was very old and feeble. One day, I was ironing, when I saw Daddy and our neighbor, Pat Pasteusek, outside the window, talking very quietly. I heard Daddy say, "Let's go around to the other side of the house." I wondered what was going on.... so I followed them from window to window. I saw Pat put a rope on Spot's neck. And I flew out of the house, screaming, "No! No! No!" I fell on the ground and grabbed Spot around the neck and started crying.

Daddy was about to cry, too. He said, "Honey, he's dying, and he's hurting. It's the best thing we can do for him."

I said, "But Daddy, I can't stand the thought of him knowing what you are going to do." So, they took the rope off his neck.

The next morning, Spot was dead. It was just time for him to go.

...an education...that never ended...

Chapter 4

PIPE-LINER'S WIFE

Pipeline construction consists of many different areas of work. What Western Pipe Coating did was to coat the pipe in a tar-like material called creosote, then wrap it with heavy paper. Often, it was done in a yard, and the pipe was then carried out to the site where it would be welded into a long line.

Other times, the coating and wrapping was done after the pipeline had been strung out and welded together. That saved going back to 'patch' the welds that had to be done in the first method.

The time length of a job depended on the size of the pipe, and the number of miles of pipe involved. Most of the time, a job consisted of a matter of weeks in one place, before moving ahead, to a closer location to where the line was being laid.

Bill was a hard worker, and his bosses liked him. They asked him to go along with them when the job at Healdton was finished. The time came for him to choose between going home and hunting for another job, or following the pipeline wherever it led. All the other boys went back home.

It wasn't an easy decision to move away from our families at home for the unknown. But he liked that kind of work, as well as the people. Still, I didn't know it was going to be a way of life for us when we moved to Lawrenceville, Illinois. I had an education in front of me that never ended.

In Healdton, the housing had been arranged before we arrived. In Lawrenceville, it was a different matter. We faced the first of many routines of hunting for a place to live. I was getting heavy in my pregnancy, and the trip had worn me out. By the time we found that horrible little house, I didn't argue.

There was the beginning of a bathroom in one corner of the room that served as living room, dining room, kitchen and bedroom. There were no walls around the commode, which we had to look at while we ate.

Speaking of eating, the move had broke us completely, and it was a while until pay day. We didn't know Herschel or Cecil or Peewee well enough to ask for a loan. So, finally, we had one can of corn to split between the two of us.... then nothing until payday another 24 hours away. That was all that we had in the house. No bread. No milk. That was my first time to be hungry. It would NOT be the last!

The wall was covered in a huge pattern of leaves that crossed each other in a design that could only be interpreted as skunks. Bill got up very, very early in the morning, and went to work. I was left alone until dark, in that one room, with no family, or friends. I still didn't know any wives at that point. I cried all day.

Our social life, after a payday, consisted of going down to a drugstore if Bill got off work before it closed.

If that was what it meant to grow up, I wished I could have stayed a kid all my life. I wanted my Mama.

The job was not nearly done. My baby was due the first part of November, less than a month away. I didn't want to have him / her in a strange hospital, with a strange doctor in Illinois. I decided I was going home, even though Bill wanted to stay where he was and finish that job. And if I was going, I needed to get on my way.

Bill took me to the little train station, helped me aboard with my huge bag, and we said goodbye. So far, so good. The trip began okay, except that I was already tired. Then, we arrived in St. Louis, where I had to change trains.

I had never seen a terminal like that before, and I have never seen one since: All the trains pulled straight into the station, engine first, like the spokes of a wheel. I had to walk from the passenger car at the rear, all the way to the station. Then, I had to go to another gate, and walk the length of another train back to that passenger car.

All that distance, there was nobody around to help me.... no Red Caps.... no helpful gentlemen. It was just me, an 8+ months pregnant girl with a heavy suitcase. It was sheer torture.

I had come a long way from that 'romantic wedding'..... but I was just getting started.

...something besides a stomach ache...

Chapter 5

MOTHERHOOD

There was never a mother happier to have her baby girl back home than my Mama was, when she and daddy met me at the depot in Wichita Falls. And there was never a baby girl that was happier to see her Mama. Neither of us remembered any of the anger or hurt feelings.

I had left Illinois the previous Sunday and arrived home on Tuesday. I collapsed, willing to allow Mama and Daddy to wait on me hand and foot. It was good to be taken care of, and to sleep in my OWN bed....

That Friday, Mama made corned beef and cabbage.... one of my very favorite foods. It was the best food I had eaten since leaving my folks and Bill's behind. Those two women were good cooks. I had not yet learned the skill of putting a meal on the table.

Saturday morning, I woke up feeling a little strange. Mama said I was needing more rest, and for me to go back to bed. I didn't argue.

I always loved for Rupert and Lillian to come see us. Their visits were always a surprise. That day, I got out of bed when they came in, then excused myself. I told mama I had a stomach ache. She said it had to have been that cabbage, and she should have known better than to let me have it.

The stomach ache got worse.....

Mama thought maybe she should call my Dr. Collins. Before she had a chance, Veneta came in. She had just learned to drive, and that was her first time to drive alone. She hadn't seen me since I got home, and just decided to drop by.

By then, I knew something besides a stomach ache was happening to me. We couldn't get the men's attention, and Mama was in no shape to drive me to the hospital. But she and Veneta put me in the back seat, and Veneta got behind the steering wheel of her car, for the second time..... Lillian told Mama not to worry, that she would take care of lunch.

Maybe I have never bragged about my sister-in-law aloud, but I will do it now.... That girl drove as fast as traffic would allow, and did a beautiful job of it.

Lying in the back seat, I was in a dream world. I could hear Mama and Veneta talking nervously..... but from out of nowhere, I heard a blood-curdling scream. I didn't know who it was, and it made me mad for somebody else to be screaming, when I was the one hurting......

I don't remember being taken out of the car. I just remember nurses trying to hold my baby back from being born, because the doctor was not there. All I could hear was them yelling at me "DON'T PUSH!!!!!" And all I wanted to do was PUSH!!!!!

It was over very quickly..... and I had the most beautiful little boy that had ever been born.

I know it's hard for young people to grasp how difficult it was back then to reach somebody across the country. Phones were not standard equipment, and we never lived in one place long enough to get one.

I did have the phone number of the company, but it was the weekend. Then, Bill was out on a job, and the bookkeeper didn't think it was important enough to go out to tell him. So my baby was two days old before Bill knew he had been born.

Bill and I had not been able to agree on a name if I had a boy. If it was a girl, it was going to be Hope Elaine.

For a boy, I wanted to name him Jimmy Burton, after the two grandfathers. But Bill was set on Billy Dean. I would not accept that, even though I liked the name. I had never dated Billy Dean James, but we joked around together, and I didn't want him to think I was naming a baby after him!

It came time for me to leave the hospital. Daddy came after me. But I could not be dismissed until the baby was named. I told Daddy my dilemma. In a flash, he said, "Let's name him Cecil."

I saw that it was important to him, so I agreed. We chose the Joe, just because it went well with the name. So, Cecil Joe Gilmore was named. And the other names were stored for future use.... except Billy Dean!

...a five gallon bucket of frog legs......

Chapter 6

ARCHER CITY

Cecil was 6 weeks old when the job was over in Illinois, and Bill came home. I don't remember what took place during the next month or so. But I do recall that Herschel and Cecil Carey both came back to Iowa Park afterward, because they came to my folk's house to see me and the baby. Mama invited them to dinner, and they accepted. So that was when I really became acquainted with the two of them.

They had left their trailer houses in Iowa Park, and had returned to move them. Their reasons for leaving them behind sometimes, and moving them to job locations other times, was never clear to me. But they did that a lot.

I know we moved to Archer City, Texas the end of 1950, when Cecil was a baby. There, we lived across the street from the Baptist Church. Bill learned that his old friend from school (before I moved to Iowa Park) was living in Archer City. He found Bobby Roderick, and we developed a friendship with him and Peggy, along with the rest of Bobby's family.

The guys began going frog hunting, almost every night. They would sometimes come in with a 5 gallon bucket of Frog Legs. They took them to Bobby's mother. She would clean them, and put them into the freezer. That was what prevented the legs from jumping out of the skillet when they were cooked.

Before freezers were standard home appliances, we had watched our mothers fry frog legs, and were fascinated when they jumped. Our mamas weren't amused, though. They got hot grease spatters quite often!

Anyway, on a Sunday afternoon, Mrs. Roderick would fry up a huge mess of frog legs for dinner. [That used to mean at Noon!] Of course, she fried potatoes, and made gravy. And we had a feast.

To me, they just tasted like chicken. But the boys thought they were eating like a king.... and I guess they were!   Just think of the price of that gourmet item today!

Neither of us remembers actually buying our first car that belonged 'just to us', but we had it at Archer City.   We know it was bought in Wichita Falls and, most likely, while we were living in Archer City. It was a 1937 Ford Coupe.

We have always remembered that time as one of the best in our young lives. A half a century later, Peggy and Bobby Roderick would become a part of our Old Friends group, and the story would be repeated about the frogs.

Peggy died unexpectedly a few years ago.

I stayed in Archer City while Bill went with some of the other men to brief jobs in Bowie, Olney and Chico, staying in motels. None were long enough to justify a move.

From Archer City, we moved to Haskell, Texas. We weren't there very long. All I remember is living in a small house with a very nice landlady. I got very sick with the flu. Right in the middle of it, we had to move on. I couldn't clean up behind us, and it really upset me. That woman just babied me, and said, "Now, don't you worry about it. I don't mind cleaning it after you are gone."

Bill gave her a few dollars extra. But just imagine the cost of leaving a place dirty these days..... the first and last months rent and no refund!!!

Chapter 7

TRINIDAD

S ince it was becoming obvious that we would be traveling with the company for some time to come, we were encouraged to buy a trailer house. We found a very small, old one, and bought it. We parked it down beside the Gilmore's home, and moved in. We must have lived there at least a week or two before we were told we would be going to Trinidad, Colorado in March of 1951.

As became the standard practice, Bill drove equipment to the job site. And I would travel with someone else, until later, when we had our own car. This trip, Peewee Vaughan would pull our trailer, and I would ride with his wife. So, the men went on, and I stayed a few days with Mama and Daddy.

Although we didn't know each other at the time, Ruth Vaughan came to the folks' house, and picked me up. She had left Dennis in Humboldt, Kansas, their hometown, to go to school, as he always did during the school year. He lived with Ruth and Peewee during the summers.

Ruth and I visited all the way, and she fell in love with Cecil Joe. It was the beginning of a 'family' relationship that lasted through their entire lives, and continues to this day, through Dennis.

When we reached Trinidad, I discovered that we didn't have that cute, tiny trailer house..... Peewee had a wreck with it, on U.S. 287, southeast of Amarillo. Our belongings were all piled into the back of a pickup, and battery acid had spilled on them. So, that was the second loss of possessions in our young life together.

Trinidad, Colorado was like moving to another country. It's beautiful now, but then it was a nasty coal town. Half the population was Mexican, and the other half Italian.... well, not quite. But it sure seemed like it.

We lived in a neat old home where two apartments had been created upstairs. The landlady was a sweet old woman who lived downstairs. In the other apartment, there was an Italian boy and his Mexican wife. Their favorite sport was fighting. That's where I learned words like "Greaser" and "Spic."

When it got too loud, the landlady would stroll upstairs, sweetly get the boy by the arm, and say, "Now, you just go on home to your mama, until you sober up. Then you come back tomorrow. You go on, now!" She would lead him down the stairs, and he would leave. The next day, he would come back and apologize to her.

I wish I could remember her name. Once, we went to the local Baptist Church with her. She had come from Arkansas, so she was used to the Southern Baptist Church, as we were. But all they had at that time in Colorado was the Northern Baptist Church.

It really took me by surprise for the sermon to be a formal lecture, and all the singing to be rehearsed, and sung by the choir, rather than the preaching and impromptu singing we were used to. On our walk home, she asked us what we thought. I cautiously said, "It was different".

She just smiled, and said, "Well, honey, you know it's always colder in the north!"

Ruth and Peewee lived in a real house, there. We spent a lot of time with them. That was when they began begging us to let them have Cecil. They told us we could have other children, and they couldn't.

For a while, I thought they were just kidding. No doubt they really loved him, and were wanting to keep him day after day, even after that precious little Dennis came out. I thought he was the cutest little boy I had ever seen. And surely, Ruth and Peewee didn't need another child.

I later learned they were quite serious. So, Cecil could have been Dennis's brother! And I could have owned the company! Instead, they later adopted siblings, Daryl, Donnie and Debbie, each as they were born to the same mother.

Cecil was just 4 months old when he said his first word..... "bye bye" several times, while waving at us. The first time, I was walking out of the room, and just told him, "Bye bye," and he repeated it. I ran downstairs and got the landlady. He said it again, and just laughed like it was such a game. Then, just as suddenly as he started it, he quit. Nobody except those who heard him would ever believe it.

Two months later, he was learning to walk. Nobody argued about that! Ruth and Peewee took credit for it, and it probably was due to their constant playing with him, walking him back and forth between the two of them.

We also became well acquainted with Herschel and Ginny there. Harry Dean was 4 years old, and a holy terror. I had been told about him, but had not witnessed his behavior first hand, until then.

We were visiting with them one night, when Harry Dean spit on Ginny, and then hit her. When she tried to scold him, Herschel told him that his mama couldn't touch him, and he could do it again. So, he did.

Ginny told Herschel, "One of these days, I'm going to leave you." Herschel smirked, "Hell! I couldn't melt you and pour you out the door!"

I told Ginny, "Come on! I will help you pack! You don't have to take this!" But Ginny just sat there, with her head down, crying.

Bill and I just shook our heads, and got up and left. That was just the first of many similar episodes.

The other memorable thing about living at Trinidad was the trip to Raton, New Mexico. Going over the Raton Pass now is a breeze. All the hair-pin curves have been removed, the road widened, and guard-rails installed. But in 1951, it was a narrow, winding road, with nothing to keep you from dropping over the side to the river below.... a long, long way below! It wasn't a trip for the faint of heart.... and I was faint of heart!

I don't recall leaving Trinidad. It seemed that we lived there for a year, but it was actually only until May. I believe we went home between jobs, from there. I could be wrong.....

Chapter 8

MOVING ON

From this point on, we moved so often, to so many places that it's very hard to remember all of them, or the correct order of the moves. Bill and I do not even agree on a lot of it. This will be recorded chronologically to the best of my ability.

The next move must have been to Iola, Kansas. We lived downstairs in a duplex, with a front porch around two sides. I had a "leash and halter" for Cecil, which I attached to the porch railing, so he could play.

Those used to be made for small children, and still should be. They allowed a toddler to roam without getting away from you, and made walking easier than having his arm in the air with somebody holding his hand. Somebody should re-introduce it.

Funny the things one remembers about previous years..... Both Bill and I talk about discovering foot-long hotdogs at a little stand in Iola. We loved them, and often had them as our meals. We still taste them after more than half a century!

We experienced our first flood at Iola, when Caney Creek overflowed into the town. Water was up into many homes, but the one we were living in was on high ground.

From Iola, we went to Wichita, Kansas. Glen and Marvel lived there, and I was looking forward to being with my brother. But I thought Marvel disapproved of our life style..... living in a cheap motel unit on the other side of town.

Glen Jr. loved coming to see us. He was old enough to get on the bus and ride across town. But he was only allowed to do that a couple of times. I had my feelings hurt, big time. When we left, we didn't call them. And that upset Marvel.

We didn't become really good friends until Glen got sick, many, many years later. I've always been sorry that we lost that time together.

I remember Wichita for one more reason, named Harry Dean. Ginny and I had gone to town in my car, and in the middle of downtown, it died. She got out to go call for help. Harry Dean was being his typical self, and bothering Cecil Joe, who was trying to sleep. I told him several times to behave. Finally, I threatened to spank him.

He said, "You don't dare touch me. I'll tell my daddy!" I turned around in the seat and looked that 5 year old straight in the eye and said, "Yes, but after you tell your daddy, I'll catch you by yourself and beat the hell out of you!"

His eyes got big, and he sat down. I never had any more trouble out of him, and even though Ginny didn't know what had taken place, she often would ask me to make him behave.....If Herschel only knew!

Our next stop was Medicine Lodge, Kansas. That town was famous for Carrie Nation.... the woman who took an ax and entered bars, chopping them up! That's one way to fight booze!!!

But we remember Medicine Lodge for two major events. For one thing, it was the place we got our first dog. A drunk had bought him the day before.... and decided when he sobered up that he didn't want a dog. So, he gave him to us. That's how we acquired Junior.

Then, at the other end of memory scale, something not so pleasant: A snowstorm shut down the job. Bill had ridden to work with an older friend, Jim Hunt. Although it was payday, Sinclair, the Bookkeeper-CPA, didn't have the checks ready. So, Jim and Bill decided to while the time away at the pool hall.

From the combination of the storm, and the fact that Jim had only one eye, an approaching train was not seen. Back then, the use of railroad crossing arms and flashing lights was limited to large cities, and most crossings were marked only with a wooden sign. Neither of them heard a whistle.

Jim pulled up on the tracks. Bill looked toward the driver's side.... then as he turned back to his own window, the engine was on top of them!

I wasn't expecting Bill home in the middle of the afternoon, but some men brought him in, kind of supporting him. He was ashy white, and it scared me. When I asked him what had happened, he answered in a very flat, monotone, "A train hit us."

He repeated those words over and over. I first thought he was joking. But then, he lay down on the bed, and asked, "Honey, am I dreaming, or did a train hit us?" During the night, he woke me several times with the same question. Of course, today, I would know that he was suffering from shock. But then, I didn't know what was wrong with him.

The story was told to me that the train knocked the truck up over the electric lines, and it landed 50 feet away, on its' wheels. Bill's door came open, and he fell out. Jim fell on top of him.

Jim was taken to the hospital with minor injuries. Nobody knew Bill was hurt, since he didn't have a scratch on him.

At the time, we thought Jim was an old man. Now we know he could not have been much over 50. He was released the next day.

The miracle is that neither of them was killed.

From Medicine Lodge, we went to Cleveland, Oklahoma. Bill and I have different versions of exactly what happened at Cleveland. We agree that Herschel was taking advantage of him being on straight time. Even though Bill was a foreman on the job, Herschel was using him as his personal valet after work. Late one evening, I went to Herschel's house to find out why Bill wasn't home. I found him washing Herschel's car. I exploded, and it was heard in the next county. I told Bill I had had enough of his being a whipping boy, and I was going home.... he could go with me, if he wanted to!

Bill has forgotten that episode, and blames his quitting on the fact that Herschel docked his pay for one day that he was sick, after him working more than 70 hours a week on a regular basis.

Both happened. Peewee heard about it, and begged us to re-consider. But we had had enough.

Before we left Cleveland, Daddy asked us to go to the Skelly office in Tulsa, to see his friend. And the man made an offer to Bill to go to work for Skelly.

Then, we packed up, and headed for home.

Chapter 9

MONAHANS

At home once more, we spent just a few days visiting with our folks before starting on a new adventure, to a new life...

Bill had been hired by Skelly, but the only opening for a new man was in Monahans, Texas. Nobody else wanted the position. We knew that Bill could handle it, and were full of anticipation as we left on that journey across the state.

We reached Monahans on a Friday, and located the plant. Bill went into the office to get his assignment, while I waited in the car with Cecil. When he came out, he was a little perplexed, showing me a paper that he had to mail home to his daddy, before he could start to work for the company.

Even though he had been working on the pipeline for almost 3 years, and was a father, he had to have a minor's release before he could be officially hired by Skelly, because he was not 21 years old.

After the letter was dropped into the post office slot, we began hunting a place to live. It soon became obvious that our lifestyle would be lowered even more than the dumpy little motels we had learned to endure. There was literally nothing to live in anywhere in the area, except one empty barracks, with no furniture, and one-inch gaps between the siding boards that had no inner walls.

As we sat in our little '37 Ford Coupe, trying to absorb the reality of Monahans, a sand storm blew in. We had heard about sand storms in West Texas.... but we had no earthly idea of what a sand storm really was.

Suddenly we were engulfed in a solid wall of sand around the car that seeped in every little crack. At times, even the sunlight seemed to be gone, and only a golden haze allowed each of us to see the outline of the other. Two terrified kids and a baby, trapped in a small car, alone in the middle of the desert. One of them suffered from claustrophobia.

The other one said, "For two cents, I would go home."

And I answered, "I have not lost a damned thing here!"

Chapter 10

HOME AGAIN

Talk about two whipped pups, we were a pair! The road home was a lot farther than it had been to Monahans. And having to tell Daddy that we were not the pioneers that he had been.. It was rough.

Mama and Daddy both begged us to leave Cecil with them, and go back. We had beat the Minor's Release home, so we had a few days to change our mind. But neither of us could endure the thought of all that sand again. We had the pitted windshield of our 37 Ford coupe to show what we had been through. But we broke Daddy's heart.

In later years, we realized that we should have been more willing to suffer for a good position with a good company. But at the time, it just was not worth the sacrifice.

Bill went to work in the oil field at home. We rented a brand new little house on the south side of the railroad tracks, just off of Victoria, near the elevator that Bobby Johnson later erected.

While we were living in that house, Peewee Vaughan came to see us. He put his beer in our refrigerator. A little later, Bill and Veneta came in. For some reason, Veneta looked in the refrigerator. She was so indignant that we had beer in it, that she stormed out. Bill Glasgow was embarrassed, but followed her.

We later learned that he went to the liquor store, and bought a 6-pack of beer. He took it home, and put it in the refrigerator.... and told Veneta that it was staying there, and she had better not touch it! She had to look at that beer every time she opened the door, until she learned that it was not going to contaminate the food, or their souls!

At some point, Lillie and Berry had bought the house on the hill above Mama and Daddy, next to the Sullivan home, beside the Duke's and Birk's 'mansions'. It had been made into a duplex.

They had it rented out, with the idea of moving back to Texas to be near Mama and Daddy. The renters of one half moved out, and we decided to move into it. It was larger than the little house, with lots of outdoor space around it, besides being next to the folks.

Speedy had gone back to the service when the war in Korea began. Now, he was home again, too. He and Bill were inseparable, as they worked together during the day.... or night shift.... and then he ate all his meals with us. That's when he became a part of our family.

We renewed old friendships with a lot of the kids we went to school with. Pete and Margaret Koonce, Delbert and Noralene Catlin, Jimmy and Nona Arnold, LaVern and her husband Bill Harrington, Joyce and Eugene Williams, among others. And we were happy there. That little duplex became the meeting place for many people.

At times, Bill and Speedy worked out of town, still in the oil fields. Once, while they were staying in a motel in Throckmorton, Texas, Bill's brother Bud, Joyce Williams, and I went down to see them on a Sunday. They were not in their room, but the motel operator gave us a key, so we could wait for them to come back.

I don't remember which one had the bright idea, but all of a sudden, the three of us began gathering their clothes and effects, right down to their toothbrushes, and loaded them into Bud's car. Then we drove to a spot where we could see them when they returned. But Joyce had to use a bathroom, so we left for a while.

When we got back, Billy Joe and Speedy were coming out of the office, headed for their car, with mad looks on their faces. We drove up just in time...they told us they had been robbed, and were going to get the police! It took us a while to convince them that was not necessary.

Gee.... anybody that can't take a little joke!

Bill did think he had a good sense of humor. He really loved to jump out of hiding, and scare me. At the time, we had an elderly neighbor, who was a bit demented. She was in the habit of opening the door and walking in.

One day, Bill came in from work while I was gone to the store. He went on to the bathroom for his shower. When he heard the door, he waited until the footsteps got into the little hall. Then he jumped out and yelled, "BOO!!!"

Of course, he retreated, when he saw our neighbor woman standing there, giggling…..She must have finally left, or he would have had the longest shower in history.

Now, the rest of my children may have been unplanned.... but Jimmy can't say that. He was certainly planned by one of us! I wanted my children close together, and Bill had promised that we would have another baby when Cecil was 2. Then, he reneged.... and said 2 ½. But when it was time for me to try to get pregnant, he reneged again.

One night, Bill and LaVern Harrington were with us. I went to the closet to get a coat to show LaVern, even though it was still summertime. In the pocket, was a huge box of condoms. We both began to laugh. And I told LaVern, "This time next month, I will be pregnant!"

The next day, I took the condoms out of their wrappers very carefully, and punched a little hole in each one, before replacing it in its wrapper. No less than 6 weeks later, I was pregnant.... though back then, a woman had to be in her 3rd month before being positive about pregnancy.

Aha! May 13th, 1953, we pulled out that name I had picked, and dubbed our new little boy Jimmy Burton Gilmore.

Jimbo soon became known for his golden curls. Wherever we went, people would ask me, "When are you going to cut that Boy's hair? Finally, in spite of my tears, he had his first haircut. Then, everybody cried, "Why did you cut that Baby's hair?"

More than fifty years later, I still sometimes see Jim's curls...but the gold has become a little rusted......that is, where it isn't silver...

...a freight train...roaring into my house...

Chapter 11

TORNADO

I don't remember the names of the couple in the other side of our house. We had become friends, which was a good thing, since we shared a common bathroom in the center of the house.

In a society where people feel deprived if they have to share a bathroom with their children, and many homes have bathrooms for every bedroom....and bathrooms are the size of many homes we lived in....it is no doubt hard for young people to understand that we were fortunate to be sharing a bathroom.

Hotels and rooming houses had a single bathroom in those days, and residents all had to take turns for a bath, or to use the toilet. But it was far advanced from the out house, and a wash tub in the kitchen floor for a bath. So, sharing a bath with a single family was no problem at all.

It was a nice evening. Jimmy and Nona Arnold wanted to go to the movies, and asked if we would baby-sit with their baby boy who was born just about the same time as our Jimmy. Of course, I said yes.

Then, the other couple asked if it was okay if they left their baby sleeping in their side of the house while they went down to my parents house to pay their rent. And, again, I said yes.

Bill decided to go to the store for something....

I didn't even see the clouds. All of a sudden, a freight train could be heard, roaring into my house. Things started moving. I got Cecil, Jimmy, and the Arnold's baby all into the front bedroom together, then made my way through the bathroom, through the kitchen of the other apartment, into a small bedroom in the back, and picked up the neighbor's baby.

As I started on the return trip through the kitchen, the window blew in on me. Fortunately, neither the baby nor I were cut.

There was a swinging door between the kitchen and the next room that led to the bathroom. The door kept hitting me, until finally I got with it, as it swung the opposite direction. I was almost to the bathroom door when an ironing board flew across the room onto me. Still, I held that baby close, and he wasn't even crying.

Once I got into our side of the house, it was a little calmer. I put the neighbor baby on the bed with the others. At least, we had a phone. I called Mama and Daddy. Although their house was just a few hundred feet away, they didn't know anything had happened.

Bill had returned from town, and was standing in the garage, waiting for the rain to stop, just a few feet from the back of the house to the north. He didn't realize a tornado had hit the house, either.

People came rushing in. It was then that we began to learn the full story. The roof was gone from the entire house, with the exception of that room where I had put all the babies. The structural reason was that there was a valley in the roof over that room that had more rafters than the flat roof. I didn't know all that when I put the children in there....but God did.

In the midst of the confusion, in total darkness, a baby was crying. Jimmy and Nona came in from their movie. Jimmy heard the baby, and felt his way to the bedroom, saying, "It's okay, honey. Daddy's going to get you." He picked the baby up and made his way out to his car, where Nona was waiting.

Just as they were about to back out, I discovered that he had picked up MY Jimmy! I ran out the door, screaming...."You've got my baby!!!" And instead of tears, we all began to laugh.

The freak tornado had come from the north, instead of the west, as usual. It had destroyed a home near the cemetery, killing a woman. Then it had bounced around, hitting not only our house, but the servants' house at the Duke residence, two houses away.

There was a young black couple living there, with their two children. I felt so sorry for that girl, as she told me, "I don't know what we are going to do. I don't want to raise my children in nigger town..." We both knew that was where they would have to go.

The Red Cross sent a volunteer to see what we needed. I don't recall them actually doing anything for us. The house was quickly repaired by somebody. And we thanked God that we were all alive.

I would endure two more tornadoes in the following years, but each from a distance, rather than in my home. One was enough!

...brown stuff in the jar...

Chapter 12

SASKATOON

Jimmy was just two weeks old when the lure of the pipeline disrupted that peaceful life at home, once again, for a job in Saskatoon, Saskatchewan, Canada in May, 1953. Peewee made Bill an offer he couldn't refuse....$100 a week as foreman, and the promise that Herschel would not repeat the previous overbearing offenses.

It was not an easy decision. We liked our house, and didn't want to give it up. Our friends, Delbert and Noralene Catlin were looking for a place to live at the time, so we arranged for them to move in, leaving our furniture in the house. By the time we would return, they would find a place of their own.

Bill liked working in the oilfield with all his old friends, especially Speedy. He asked Speedy to go with us, but being afraid that he wouldn't have a job, Speedy declined.

Our last stop before leaving Iowa Park was my parents' home. As we were telling them goodbye, Speedy drove up, one more time. He followed us to the car, and Bill told him it still wasn't too late to change his mind. But he just couldn't make that decision. He hung on the window until we just had to go. It was really hard to leave him behind, looking like a lost puppy.

We couldn't understand why our parents were worried about us making that trip. After all, we were 20 years old, and weren't afraid of the world. So we set out on U.S. 83, across our country. We were in a 'new car'.... a 1946 Ford coupe. So, why worry?

It never occurred to us that it should be a three day trip to Canada. We didn't even consider getting a motel, at any point. We just kept driving. Bill got sick, and couldn't drive for very long at a time.

I ended up driving most of the way across Nebraska, in a flood. There were tall stakes at the edge of the highway, to show the road in the water. I guess that meant it had been that way a while. Or, it was going to be there a while longer!

If a highway is covered with water now, it's closed. But vehicles were built higher off the ground then, to accommodate high water and deep ruts.

By South Dakota, the rains stopped. Then, the pavement ended. We drove and drove and drove, wondering if we had missed our road.... then, finally, there would be a highway sign, letting us know that we were still on U.S. 83.

We stopped only to eat. To make feeding Jimmy simpler, we just started feeding him plain milk, out of a milk bottle. We didn't even heat it. He gobbled it up! And, he never had colic.

I thought of all the formulas we had tried with poor little Cecil, and how sick he had been as a baby. If we had only been as careless with him as we were with Jimmy, just maybe..... oh, well.

We did invest in those expensive, new disposable diapers. The only problem was that, as soon as they got wet, they tore up. And the safety pins were hard to push through them. But it was better than having a bucket of dirty diapers in the car.

You haven't lived unless you have washed dirty cloth diapers, by hand.... then, put them in a large pot on the stove, or fire, to boil. There were no short cuts.... or the baby paid with a sore bottom. And you don't want to live with a baby that has a sore bottom!

But I digress!

Somewhere between the Canadian border and Regina, the road was paved again. And, it seemed like God turned the lights on, so we could see better.

Herschel and Ginny must have had a telephone. Otherwise, I don't know how we would have known where they lived. But we went straight to their house, when we reached Saskatoon. We visited a while, then Herschel said, "Well, I don't mean to be rude, but we've got to go to bed! Four o'clock comes early!"

Bill and I looked at each other with questions on our faces. The sun was still shining outside. Then Herschel pointed to the clock, and it was 10:00pm!

We went to a hotel, and though it was daylight, we had no trouble sleeping, after some 30 hours of straight driving. I don't remember if Bill went to work at 4 a.m., or not! Most likely, he helped me find a place to live, since I had two babies.

For a short while, we lived in an upstairs apartment in Saskatoon. But the stairs were steep, and we didn't like the landlady. So, we moved into an old 'Tourist Court'... the pre-runner of modern day motels...in the suburb of Sutherland. It was being rented to permanent residents. It wasn't as nice as the apartment, but Cecil had room to play, and we had more privacy.

In the adjacent unit, there was an old woman who still sounded very British. A lot of people in the area were directly from Europe. We visited outside a few times. Then, she asked me to come in to her house, and look at her new Ice Box. Of course, I thought she meant a refrigerator, as many people still called them Ice Boxes. But, sure enough, there was a brand new Ice Box.... in 1953. I respectfully admired it. Then, the old woman said, "Oh, honey! It is SO much better than a DUG OUT!" I felt like I had returned to the Dark Ages.

Then, we found another apartment, with friendly people. We soon met neighbors on both sides, and across the street. There were stores nearby, and when I walked down the sidewalk, people I didn't recognize would say, "Hi, Tex!" So, the word had gotten around that those 'new people' were from Texas.

A young woman about my age visited me a lot. She was from Wales, and lived across the street. One day, she came in, very excited, and asked me to come over to her house, to see her new automatic washing machine.

I was very impressed that automatic washers had reached Canada. That was one thing I really would like to have. And, I had forgotten the incident involving the Ice Box. So, I was just as amazed when I saw a brand new wringer washing machine. To her, it was automatic, because she didn't have to wash the clothes by hand!

I don't know why, unless there was a law, but the guys didn't work on Sunday. It became kind of expected that our whole gang would pack a lunch, and go to a park together every week. Saskatoon was a beautiful city, with a river running through it, and lots of bridges crossing it.... I believe there were five of them, and they were all objects of beauty. There were parks everywhere. So, our Sundays were always fun.

Ice tea was foreign to Canadians. And when our neighbors saw all of us packing our food into the trunk, always with a gallon jar of tea, they were puzzled. Finally, one came up and asked us, "What's that brown stuff in the jar?" So, we gave him a taste, to prove we weren't carrying booze to our picnic!

We really enjoyed the time we were there, and all the people we met.... not only locals, but those employees that we had not known before. One of those was a boy from Coffeeville, Kansas, by the name of Dick Wooldridge.

Dick had recently divorced. He met a Canadian girl named Ann..... I don't remember her last name. But after we went back to the States, she joined him, and they got married.

We were sorry when the job was over. We liked the long days, when we could come out of a late movie, and the sun would be high in the sky, and when dark finally arrived, the Northern Lights glowed like it was Christmas. It was probably the most pleasant place we ever lived, while on the pipeline.

Chapter 13

IOWA TO IOWA PARK

We must have bought a lot of junk in Canada, because our little Coupe was loaded to the maximum when we left Saskatoon. Dick Wooldridge drove with us, and took Cecil with him, to give us more room for Jimmy to lie down.

Our next stop would be Atlantic, Iowa. We remember that town mainly as the place we bought our fabulous 1950 chartreuse and black Crestliner Ford, the first of our memorable cars that we wish we still had. Oh, Wow! Personality Plus! Leather seats, yet! We were up town!

Atlantic was also the place that my 'writing' began. We couldn't get a place to live, because we would not be permanent, we had children and a dog. The motel did get a bit crowded. I wrote my first "Letter to the Editor" and sent it to the local paper.

The subject was that situation that all of us experienced. I said we could get rid of our pets, but we would really like to keep our kids. We moved into a town, and all the prices went up, not only for motel rooms, but on food, as well. Cafes printed two menus… one for locals, and one for us. While we were there, we boosted their economy.

My letter was put on the Editorial page, in a full column by the editor supporting what I had said. Although I signed it "A Pipeliner's Wife", word soon got around that I had written it. The positive support I received led to my other items that were published over the years. That first clipping, and many others, are somewhere in my attic, or the garage…. probably falling apart now!

We finally found a very large trailer house that was offered on a temporary basis, due to my letter. It sat in the back yard of the owners, carnival people, who left their catalogs in the bookcases.

We had some very interesting reading material, and learned a lot about WHY you can't knock down those bowling pins when you hit them squarely in the center…. along with a lot of other carnival secrets. Needless to say, it probably saved us a lot of money in future years!!!

I don't remember how long we stayed in Atlantic, but it was not very long. The trip home also is gone from my memory. I do know that Bill went back to Storm Lake, Iowa, and I stayed home.

I worked for a short period as a carhop for Skeet Eddins and her first husband, when they opened a drive-in near Probst's Station on the old highway. I was just helping out a friend, rather than trying to earn money. It was fun, as I knew everybody, and everybody knew me. I must have been leaving the two babies with one of our two Mamas. For whatever reason, I only worked a few weeks.

Bill came home from Storm Lake and returned to his oilfield job, which was always waiting for him. Life returned to normal, with him and Speedy working together, and Buddy with them at meal time around our kitchen table.

It got to be a habit for Buddy to borrow our Crestliner after supper. I didn't mind for a while, but soon I got tired of driving his old clunker if I wanted to go someplace.

One night, I asked Bill not to loan the car, because I wanted it. He promised he wouldn't. After supper, as I was doing dishes, I looked out the window and saw Bill and Speedy standing in the garage. Buddy was gone….in our new car. To say that I was angry would be the understatement of the year.

I flew out the door, grabbed the keys out of Buddy's car, and threw them across the fence, as far into the field next to us as I could throw! Then I went into the house and gathered every last stitch of clothing, every personal belonging, everything that even looked like it could be my dear husband's, and threw them out the door. Then I locked the door behind them.

I got Bill's attention! Eventually, they found Buddy's keys. And, eventually, BJ wormed his way back into the house. And Speedy told the story at least 100 times, laughing his head off. But I kept my own car after that!

...another chance at life...

Chapter 14

LIFE AND DEATH

When children come along, every family has the problem of identifying the grandparents in a way the little ones can understand. In our case, my Mama and Daddy became Big Grandma and Big Grandpa. Bill's folks were Little Grandma and Little Grandpa. We don't remember how it started, but it stuck, and all through the years, even our friends adopted those nicknames, and knew which set of grandparents we were referring to. My mama wasn't really big. But Bill's mama was really LITTLE! His daddy wasn't really little, but my daddy was really TALL. It worked, and both sets were known by those names until their deaths.

We had a great Christmas, 1953, with lots of pictures taken at his parent's house. Bill and Speedy were working on the same location as they were when Speedy received the call that his daddy had died.

Little Grandpa had been sick for a long time. Finally, he allowed me to take him to the hospital, in January, 1954. Bill, Bud and Veneta were all at work. They came in that evening, and we all visited at the hospital. We left Little Grandpa laughing.

The next morning, I got the call after Bill had gone to work. I called his boss, Joe Hale. In the confusion, Bill was told to go to the hospital, instead of coming home. When he got there, he was told that his daddy was dead. He had to drive home alone, with that terrible shock. He was 21 years old.

This is supposed to just be the story of my life, fact by fact. But the fact remains that emotions become facts of life. I had not lost anybody close to me, except Sandy's daddy, since my grandpa died when I was four. Mr. Williams death didn't really affect me, and I was too young when Grandpa died to even know what it was. So, when Little Grandpa died, it whammied me, big time.

The Gilmore family met at our house for the funeral. A long lost cousin thanked me for being so nice to 'the family.'

And, who did she think I was???

Life goes on.

Veneta got pregnant for the first time. I gave her all my maternity clothes. Then, a couple of weeks later, I asked for them back!

Cecil was 3 years old. Jimmy was still a baby, 10 months old. I wanted my children close together, but I was not prepared for learning I was pregnant again, so soon! I was so sick I thought I would die.

A friend suggested that maybe that's what I got for punching holes in Bill's condoms!

Then, Bill got a call to go to Edmonton, Alberta, Canada. He left almost immediately, and was gone for several months.

I had not had morning sickness very long with the other two babies. But this was all-day sickness, every day. It was all I could do to get out of bed. Bill had asked Speedy to take care of his family, and he did his best. He and Buddy both took the babies with them a lot, so I could get some rest. Speedy swept my floors and washed my dishes, and fed the kids.

Mama and Daddy helped me, too. But they were grateful to Speedy, just as I was, for all his help. Little Grandma was taking care of Veneta.

Then, Speedy and Buddy got a job in Colorado, and it was too good an offer to turn down. So the folks had the entire burden.... and I know I was a burden!

I kept telling Dr. Clark that I knew I was carrying two babies, because one would be kicking my ribs while the other was kicking my tail bone! In 1954, the only way to tell was with an x-ray. Finally, Dr. Clark decided he had to make the x-ray, in spite of the danger, because of my huge size. I was right!!! I have that picture of my twins in my womb, more than half a century later. [It's in my cedar chest.]

When the job in Edmonton was almost over, Speedy and Buddy left their job and drove to Canada to get Bill. The three of them had an adventure on the trip home that they never forgot. Even though I wanted Bill home more quickly, I've always been glad for them, that they had that time together.

The next weeks kind of run together in my mind. The guys were back in the oil field. We bought our beautiful, large, two-bedroom New Moon trailer house, and put it in a trailer park on 9th Street in Wichita Falls. Later, we moved it to the vacant lot beside Little Grandma's house.

My babies were due on New Years Day. Veneta's baby was expected a little sooner. On December 14th, 1954, I went for a check-up. Because of my weight, and fear of complications, Dr. Clark sent me to the hospital, to induce labor. In the adjacent labor room was my sister-in-law!

Veneta had Craig that day. He weighed less than 6 pounds. Even though I couldn't see her in the adjacent labor room, I really missed the contact by way of BJ and Bill Glasgow, running back and forth, when she was gone.

The attempts to make me deliver were not working. The next day, they prepared to do a C-section, but Dr. Clark decided to try one more method of inducing labor. Whatever it was, he poured a cold liquid over my belly, and things started happening, fast and furiously, without anesthetic. It wasn't supposed to happen that way.

Both my little boys were born bottom breach, within 5 minutes of each other. The first one, we named Kelly Len. He weighed 6 lbs, 8 oz. Then, Kenny Glen, the runt, only weighed 6 lbs, 4 oz. Needless to say, my body felt like it had been through a meat grinder! Dr. Clark later joked, "It's better to have 13 pounds of two than 13 pounds of ONE!"

I didn't find that amusing, at all! Well… maybe a little….

I hesitate to this day to relate what happened to me during, and after the birth of my twins, because it is so hard to explain. From the medical view, I went into 'shock', and began 'hallucinating'. Mother was with me, and was terrified. Our pastor, Brother Reik was there, and it scared him, too.

Actually, I was about to leave my body behind. I begged God to give me another chance at life. It was an experience that I had to push into the back of my mind, because I soon learned that people thought I was crazy when I tried to talk about it.

I was told that I had to settle down, or I would have to be put in isolation. So, from the mental part of my brain, I knew I had to suppress what God was saying to me, and not tell anybody else.

I thought I would never forget what happened that day, but I did. It is just a faint memory now, not clear at all, as it was for many years. But it happened.

I did a good cover-up job, and was moved into a ward with six beds. There was Veneta, across from me! And a couple of beds down, there was my classmate, Wanzell Copeland Duggins....

Veneta went home the next morning. But Wanzell stayed. I was glad to have her company. Neither of us dreamed then that nearly fifty years later, she would become a great-aunt, through marriage, to my Karlee.

I was bothered, because when it was time for the nurses to bring the babies, they kept bringing my little Kenny Glen. I told them I wanted to see Kelly Len. They always made an excuse, like they just got mixed up, and 'next time', they would bring the right baby. After a while, I got suspicious.

Dr. Clark then came to talk to me. He said that a specialist had been with Kelly Len for several hours. But there was no possibility that he could live. He hugged me, and cried with me. It was just a matter of hours before my baby would die.

Bill had been called, but had not yet arrived at the hospital.

A nurse from Hell handed me a pan of water and wash cloth, and told me to 'get my bath'. I ignored her. She turned around, and told me she didn't have all day. Then she saw a tear run down my face, and said "Well, there's nothing to cry about! If you hurt, I'll get you a pill." I answered, "Lady, if you have a pill for this hurt, I'll take it!" She still persisted in ordering me to get my bath.

Wanzell walked up to her, and told her, in no uncertain terms, to leave me alone. Then she walked down to the desk and reported the nurse. I think they sent her back to where she came from....... I know I suggested that she to go there.....

Almost immediately, I was moved into a private room, even though I wanted to stay in the ward. But it was best that we were alone when Bill got there, as we waited together for our baby to die. Family members and friends came in and out, all crying with us. Another day passed, before little Kelly Len gave up his fight to live.

Katy Merle asked if she could provide the little burial clothes for our baby, and we gratefully said yes. Somehow, we made funeral plans.

I was taken home, but wasn't allowed to go to the funeral. James Hair sang. I stayed home, and held my precious Kenny Glen.

Daddy wouldn't leave my side. He cried more than anybody else, including me.

Some chapters in life just don't have a lot of humor in them.

Thank God, we still had Kenny Glen. He brought a double dose of joy into our lives.

...trying to wake up from a terrible dream...

Chapter 15

EXPERIENCE

The year of 1955 would prove to be most enlightening to two young kids who thought they knew it all. The old adage, "experience is the best teacher," was about to be proven.

It was time to hit the pipeline road again. This time, we would be pulling our New Moon home. We loved our Crestliner Ford, but it was evident that it was not strong enough to tow the trailer. So, something had to be done. We had made one mistake when we bought the New Moon, using the Ford as collateral. The dealer would not release the lien so that we could trade vehicles.

Bill's friend, Teddie Treasor, had a new 1954 Buick that he was about to lose. So, it was a very simple matter to trade cars, and each of them keep making the payments. When everything was paid, we would just exchange titles. So, Teddie took our Crestliner, and we took his Buick.

The next location was Frankfort, Kansas. Speedy went with us, driving his own car. He lived with us, sleeping on the sofa-bed in the living room. He shared expenses, and that certainly was better for all concerned.

I don't remember a lot about Frankfort. Dennis has reminded me that it was there that I carried Bill's lunch to him...as Dennis said, "Enough for three men, plus a half-gallon of tea, and he ate every bit of it!"

Bill was rather known for his hefty appetite. At the time, he may have weighed 125 pounds. An inspector decided to find out exactly how much such a little guy really could eat. He offered to buy all the chicken-fried steaks Bill could hold. Back then, a chicken-fried steak was served on a platter. Of course, he had to eat the other things on the plate, too.

So, we all went to the local café. Everybody had a steak. Then Bill ordered another one. He ate it all, as we watched. On the third one, he began to slow down, and finally had to give it up!

Our next move was to Humboldt, Kansas, the headquarters of the company. Excess equipment was kept there when it was not needed. Ruth and Peewee always had a home in Humboldt, as did Cecil and Mary. Many of the other pipeliners were also from Humboldt.

Home base for the family was the farm near Humboldt, actually five miles south of Yates Center, that belonged to R.D. and Vada Sellers. They were the mother and step-father of Ruth, Cecil, Herschel and Harry Carey. We went there many times. In later years, Bill bought the old Model A truck that R.D. used on the farm when we were there.

I remained in Humboldt with the kids while Bill helped move equipment to Big Piney and Kemmerer, Wyoming, where a very large job was beginning. Then, he came back for us. He pulled the trailer with a company truck, and I followed in the Buick.

The trip had been uneventful, and we had crossed the state line between Colorado and Wyoming when Cecil wanted to ride in the truck with his daddy. I had not let him previously, because I was afraid he would distract Bill. Not only was he responsible for the truck, but pulling the trailer made it more difficult. I guess I finally decided that there was no danger. So, while we stopped for a rest, Cecil Joe climbed into the truck.

It was a warm day, and my little boys were dressed in shorts, and no shoes. The beauty of traveling with your home is that you don't have to pack. If you need something, you just go inside and get it while you are stopped.

We were traveling along U.S. 287, the highway that begins on the Gulf Coast of Texas at Port Arthur, through Beaumont, up to Corsicana, on through Fort Worth to Wichita Falls and Iowa Park. From home, it goes northward, through Amarillo, Denver, and Laramie, continuing through Yellowstone Park, out through Helena, Montana to the Canadian border.

We passed Laramie, and started into the mountain range just northwest of that city. There was one car in front of me, between our vehicles. Bill started down a very long hill toward a bridge over a river. I saw the trailer begin to swerve from side to side, faster and faster toward the bottom.

I began to scream, and stepped on the gas in the Buick, passing the other car, as those people stared in disbelief. I reached the bottom just as Bill hit the bridge. The trailer broke loose and hit the truck, turning it around, leaving it with one wheel hanging on the edge of the bridge. Then, the trailer gently rolled onto its side, across the highway.

It's impossible to re-create the scene in correct order of events. Somehow, I was out of the car, and had Cecil Joe in my arms. He had a big bruise on his head, where he had hit the windshield, but otherwise, seemed to be okay. We inspected the trailer, and saw that it was intact.

We knew that several of our gang was behind us, in vehicles that could join efforts, and lift our trailer upright. The truck was still in drivable condition. We began to relax, and tried to talk to the mass of bystanders who had gathered not only from other travelers, but also from the tiny town of Medicine Bow, where the accident occurred.

A highway patrolman showed up, and began strutting around. He insisted that, no matter what, the trailer had to be moved off of the highway, immediately. Even though we told him we had trucks coming right behind us that could do it, he called a wrecker. The wrecker driver was an idiot who hooked cables onto the underside, and pulled the floor out. Then he threw a cable across the middle, and finished demolishing our home, before our very eyes.

Then, our gang arrived. The men began gathering as much of our belongings as possible, especially our clothes, putting them into the back of the company truck that Speedy was driving. Strangers helped.

I had all I could do, just trying to take care of my three babies. Cecil was hurt far worse than we thought, and we were just too young to know to insist on calling a doctor for him. I could only imagine what it was for that four-year-old, experiencing the downward careening toward the river below. He was terrified every time we got into a car for several months afterward.

In all the confusion, our dog, Junior, was either picked up, or ran away in fright. We stayed behind when the trucks left, and looked for him as long as we could. Then we had to go on.

Junior was gone. Our home was gone. We were devastated. In the following two weeks, each time some of our people passed through, they looked again. But our Junior was never found.

How Bill ever managed to get into the driver's seat of our car, I'll never know. I could not have driven another mile. But we traveled on, trying to wake up from a terrible dream. It just couldn't get any worse. Or could it?

Three miles from our destination of Kemmerer, we drove upon a scene that is forever etched in my mind: A truck was burning…. Oh, yes. It was the truck carrying all our worldly possessions, every item of clothing we owned, as well as anything else we had.

The men were frantically trying to put out the fire, and were raking everything on to the ground. I stood and watched my only childhood treasure burn, my one and only doll. To me, she was like one of my babies, and there was nothing I could do for her.

Peewee had driven out from town as soon as he got the message. He walked over and put his arm around me, to comfort me. I passed out.

I opened my eyes, and saw that I was lying on the ground, with all the men leaning over me, trying to help. It wasn't real. I was someplace else, and all this was not really happening.

I don't remember going on into town. But we were taken to Ruth and Peewee's trailer. Where they put us, with our three children, I don't know. But we stayed with them until we found an available tourist cabin, outside of town.

There, we lived for several weeks, in one room just big enough for a regular bed, a table and chairs, and a wood stove. The toilet was out in the back. The owners loaned us some extra quilts, to put the kids on the floor at night. There simply was not another place to live, due to the huge job bringing every phase of pipelining people to the area.

Bill and Speedy were working in the pipe coating yard in Opal, about 15 miles south. Finally, they talked the owner of an old railroad house near the yard into letting us live in it. There were no windows. But it had a bedroom, 'living room' and kitchen, such as it was.

There was a huge pot-bellied stove in the center of the living room. We tried to cover the windows with blankets that people loaned, or gave us. We cooked on a camp stove that was salvaged from the fire.

There were no laundry places like those we had at home, where wringer washers and rinse tubs could be used for a fee. I had no choice. Bill would build an outside fire before he went to work, and I heated water in an old iron pot from someplace. Maybe it was already there. And I scrubbed the clothes on a rub-board, like my mama used to do, before I was born.

Winter set in. I couldn't keep enough wood in the stove to warm the house for the little boys to play. I had to keep them wrapped in blankets, on the cots we were using for beds. Oh yeah! I earned my Pioneer Woman Badge. Mama and Daddy would have been proud of me, if they had been aware of the situation.

Two of the other women that I had just recently met came over one day, to see about us. One of them picked Kenny up, and discovered that he was freezing cold. I had not realized that he wasn't warm under his covers. The women took us to their hotel room to warm up. Two angels, if ever have I encountered any.

They were not on any of the other jobs where I was, and when we moved from there, I never saw them again.

Eventually, somebody found us a great house in Diamondville, a suburb of Kemmerer, a real house, with windows and doors, a kitchen with a wood cook stove, and three bedrooms. I don't mean huge rooms like people think they have to have today. But there were little rooms that were separated by walls, and there were beds in each room. The toilet was just outside the back door. We were in heaven.

I loved getting up at 4 a.m. and cooking breakfast on that wood stove for the guys, because we had a place to live! They had to be at work at five, to start the 'dope pot' that heated the 'tar' that was used in coating the pipe.

We had a party there for Cecil's 5th birthday there, and everybody in our gang came to it. It was as festive as if it had been held in a castle.

While we were living there, Peewee and Speedy went hunting, and brought a deer to our house. They butchered the thing in my kitchen, and in the process, cut slices for me to cook at that very moment....with blood and guts everywhere. I held my breath, and fried my first piece of venison. The smell made me ill. But those men were so proud of themselves, and thought it was the best venison they had ever eaten. Ugh!!

Chapter 16

EDUCATION

I don't remember the exact reason I had to go home, but it had to do with insurance on the trailer. I took the boys, and went by train. Mama and Daddy had moved to town by then, into the house on Cash Street. We stayed with them while I tried to accomplish some miracles in financing.

The final outcome was that the dealer had the insurance written to cover only the balance of the note. So, there was no insurance, for us. In those days, there was no such thing as suing the wrecker driver who destroyed our home, or the Highway Patrol for unreasonable actions.

My childhood friend, Janette Lynskey, had just been through a traumatic divorce, and when it was time for me to go back to Wyoming, she asked if she could go with me, and we would drive her car. So, we loaded that vehicle, and started driving north, as young people always do, without stopping.

I was driving, somewhere in Colorado, at 1 a.m. when I looked down and saw that we were almost out of gasoline. I got to the next little town, but of course everything was closed. I pulled under the cover of a filling station to wait for it to open. We ran the engine off and on, as long as there was fuel. We pulled out all the clothes to bundle in. And we went to sleep.

We never knew it was morning, until a snow plow cleared the wall of natural insulation from around the station, and let the daylight into our car! It had not even been snowing when we went to sleep, but we were completely enclosed. We realized then that our lives would have been in jeopardy, if we had not stopped under the shelter of that station, and had run out of gas out on the road. The Lord at work, again!

As luck would have it, as we left that town, we passed a motel with a 'vacancy' sign, just blocks past the station where we had slept.

Again, we set out on our journey across Wyoming's southern plains, through Rock Springs, then another hundred miles on to my little house in Diamondville. But nobody was there. The house was empty. I found somebody among our people that knew the job had moved on, and the guys were 100 miles away....in Rock Springs!

We were not happy campers! But we managed to drive back, arriving after dark, at a strange place that looked like a hen house, where Bill and Speedy thought we were going to live. After one look, I found a motel until morning.

The next day, we located an upstairs apartment in slightly better condition. We lived there just a few weeks, before the job shut down. It was the coldest place I have ever been, at 12 below zero, and the wind blowing.

The men heard of another job, for another contractor, in Baker, Oregon. Several of our guys decided to go there, because they thought nobody else would be wanting to work in the dead of winter. So, we drove in a caravan, our Buick, Janette's car, Speedy's car, and Clifford and Jo Hunt, in their vehicle, to Oregon. Part of the way, the snow was plowed up higher than our cars, creating walls on each side of us.

We found a house with plenty of room, and a basement. By the time the rent was paid, we were broke. Guess what? The entire pipeline-following population from the United States thought the same thing. There was no immediate work. Bill, Clifford and Speedy went hunting, out of season. They brought back a deer, which they butchered in the basement.

There was a small grocery store within walking distance. We bought bread and milk, only. Three times a day, I cooked venison, and made gravy. The men thought we were living well. I could hardly eat it.

No matter how bleak particular times in life may be, there are always little bits of enjoyment that are remembered. In Baker, baby Kenny had to sleep on a folding cot, because he didn't have a crib. Each night, after we put him to bed and went into the adjacent living room to visit a while, he would slip out of the bed, and sidle slowly and quietly along the wall until he was in a corner of the room with us.

He would stand with his little arms glued straight down to his body, his head slightly bowed, and his little brown eyes peeking out carefully, so that we 'couldn't see' him. Everybody played the game, night after night, talking about him as if he wasn't there. Then somebody would 'discover' him, and he would be scooped up and put to bed again. That went on until he either fell asleep, or we went to bed ourselves. It was fun, and there was no need to be stern with him.

I don't know why it had not happened before that house, or why it stopped when we left there. I guess it was the location of his bed, and where we were sitting. But that's one of our favorite memories of his baby days.

The guys finally got to work a while, up in the mountains, in 40 below weather. I thought that was a perfect time to get sick, and go to the hospital. The doctor told me I needed to take better care of myself!

When I was released, we managed to come up with a cake for Kenny's 1st birthday, December 15th. Then, we decided it was time to head for Texas. We all wanted to be home for Christmas.

Another caravan, this time three vehicles, began the non-stop journey through snow-covered mountains, headed south in the dead of winter, before modern highways existed. Now, it can be considered an adventure. Then, it was just a matter of necessity.

We made it!

I should remember our arrival at home, and where we spent Christmas that year, but I don't. I do know all our Christmases were good, regardless of whether or not we had much under the tree, or where the tree happened to be.

A few days after Christmas, Speedy asked Bill to go to Miami with him, to see his brother. I told Bill we couldn't possibly ever be any more broke, and he might as well go. So, they drove the Buick down to Florida.

They got stopped in Pensacola, and were charged with driving a vehicle that was not theirs. Bill tried to explain the deal about trading cars with Teddie Treasor. They were not buying the story.

At some point, the guy in charge told them they could leave the jail, but to stay in town until they were checked out. He was confident that they wouldn't leave, since he kept their keys. He just didn't know there was a second set.

They jumped into the car and fled, like the criminals they were!

In Miami, they went deep sea fishing, living it up. Then, they returned to Iowa Park. Immediately, people from the finance company were there to pick up the Buick.

After the fact, we learned that Teddie just quit sending in the payments on the Buick, even though we had seen to it that we never were late sending him the money, regardless of what else we had to do without. By then, he was living in Arkansas. So, we went after our Ford.

We found the car wrecked. Teddie and his wife were living in a nice place, with lots of new furniture that our money had bought. And neither of them blinked an eye.

I earned my Master's Degree in the department of Trusting People. Bill failed the course, and would continue to believe that everybody was his friend. It's a trait that I both admire, and despair over, to this day!

Chapter 17

WASHINGTON TO IDAHO

The interim before returning to the pipeline is a blur to me. I know that I stayed home a while, and Bill went somewhere in the northwest, but he doesn't even remember where. Maybe it was to North Bonneville, Washington, where I joined him in 1956.

Our little boys and I flew from Wichita Falls to Lubbock, where there was a steward waiting for 'the woman with three children'. I was helped into the terminal, and the man stayed with the kids while I went to the bathroom. He handled everything, making us comfortable, until our next flight was ready. Then, he came for us, ahead of all the other passengers, and put us on the plane to Denver.

A stewardess took over from there, buckling the little ones into seats, and again making sure that we didn't need anything before she left us.

The same thing happened at Denver. That time, after we were in the air, the stewardess came back, and put each child to bed in vacant seats, where they had room to lie down. It was an overnight flight, twelve hours to Portland, Oregon. We were pampered, and fed like royalty.

Oh, for the good old days of flying! I could fly with three babies today, and never get one bit of attention, unless another passenger took pity, the way Bill and I did with a young woman on our last flight. The airlines certainly aren't concerned with any individuals. The masses are all the same. That's too bad.

Bill met us in Portland. North Bonneville is so named, as that is where the Bonneville Dam is located, across the Columbia River, between Washington and Oregon, near Portland.

We lived in a Tourist Court that sat on the very bank of the Columbia.. In fact, my back window looked out onto the dam. We could watch the salmon swim upstream, and scale the 'ladders' in the dam. It was quite a sight.

We had heard of Louie Cowsar all the time Bill had been with the company. Old pipeliners all knew each other, and sooner or later, would work together. Louie and his wife, Bess, lived in the unit next door to us, and that's when our friendship began. It took me many years to be comfortable with Bess. She was older, and appeared to be very sophisticated, maybe a little reserved. But after I got to know her, we became very close. Bill and Louie hit it off instantly.

There were various jobs going on at the same time in the area. Bill worked some at The Dalles, and Hood River, Oregon, while we lived at North Bonneville. Speedy was not on those jobs, but was with another group, maybe at Bellingham, at that time. I know the Bellingham job lasted quite some time, after we had moved on.

Our next move was to Spokane. There, we had a beautiful house, in a very nice part of town. We were there for many months, and made friends among all our neighbors. I should remember the names, but it's been too long. And I should remember more about living there, but I don't.....
The only incident I remember was Bill coming into the bedroom one day while I was ironing. He asked me for $10. I asked him what he needed it for. He told me he was going to loan it to a friend on the job. I told him I didn't know the guy. Finally, I gave it to him, and told him to kiss it goodbye, because he would not get it back. I was right. I think he hated that, worse than losing the money!

Somewhere along the line, we acquired a pickup. Neither of us remember where we got it, but we did have it at Spokane.
My brother-in-law, Berry Barnes, died at Powell, Wyoming, during that time. We went to the funeral, even though I was not well. It was good to see my whole family.

A couple of months later, my precious Grandma died, at Hammon, Oklahoma. By that time, I was in the hospital. I was heart-broken from losing her, and disturbed that I couldn't go home.

When the next job began in Twin Falls, Idaho, I had to stay behind, until I was able to travel. Bill took the little boys with him, and left them with Jo Hunt during the day. When I was released, I boarded a train for Twin Falls. It felt like my boys had been away from me for months, while it was actually about 2 weeks.

There, we lived in an old efficiency motel, where the units were all connected, end to end. We had one bedroom, a bed in the front room, a kitchenette and a bathroom, consisting of a commode and a shower stall. It wasn't bad... just small.

It was early December by then, and just like at Rock Springs, the wind blew all the time. To get to the trash cans, we had to walk all the way to the end of the motel, and then back half-way up the alley to the cans. Then, we had to return by the same long trek.

Once, while fixing a meal, I burned some stew meat. When Bill came in from work, I asked him to please take it to the trash for me. He said it was too cold outside, and I should just flush it down the toilet. I refused, telling him it would clog the toilet. We got into an argument, which ended with him scraping the scraps into the commode, and me yelling that I wasn't going to go after a plunger when it stopped up!

Speedy came in, just as the water started running across the floor. Bill was begging me, "Honey, please get the mop! Honey, go get a plunger! Honey, help me!" I just stood there and watched him, while refusing to lift a finger. Finally he said, "Speedy, go get a plunger!" And Speedy went to the office, as I was telling Bill that the manager would come back with him. Then, I heard the two men at the door. I ran into the little bedroom, shut the door, and hid.

The guy walked in, took a look at the mess and said, "Boy, it is really stopped up. What happened?" Bill answered, "I don't know. Honey, do you know what happened to the commode? Honey ??? HONEY ????"

I doubled up laughing, and stayed where I was. Then I heard Bill say, "Well, you know how kids are. One of them probably stuffed a toy into it."

Little Cecil Joe chimed in, "Huh-UH! Daddy put the garbage in the toilet! "

Cecil survived…..

Dick and Ann were also on the job at Twin Falls. We visited every day, and became like one family. By then, they had Donna, and my little boys all loved her.

Christmas came. We found an imitation fireplace, and put it on the wall of the front room, and hung stockings on it. I don't remember what our little boys got, but it was a very happy Christmas.

The job was nearing an end, and we thought we were going home. Speedy decided to leave, since the location he was on had already finished. Cecil wanted to go home with him, instead of waiting for us. We decided that he could go stay with Mama and Daddy until we got home.

It seemed that no sooner were they gone than we got word that we were moving to Pocatello. The move was completed before we hardly knew we were going. Dick and Ann were among the others that went along. We found a really nice motel with kitchenettes, around a courtyard. Our little homes were across the courtyard from each other.

Unexpectedly, I had to go to a hospital with hemorrhaging.

Everybody was very good to me. Ann kept the kids. The motel owner and his wife took over my laundry and house-keeping. My doctor was a Mormon missionary, and he acted like I was the only patient he had. He had to perform surgery, to stop the bleeding.

Bill had called home, and asked his mother to come up to help and bring Cecil back with her. But Veneta was pregnant with Cary, and Little Grandma needed to be there. So, my Mama came. I loved Little Grandma, but there's nobody like your own mama when you are sick. It was nice to have her to come home to, when I was released.

We all thought I was able to take care of myself, and my kids, with all the help I had, so I let Mama go home after a week or so. Right after she left, I developed an extremely high fever, and the bleeding began again.

I was rushed back to the hospital, where I was wrapped in wet sheets, with crushed ice packed around me, and a fan turned on. I thought I would die from the treatment to lower my temperature, which was by then 107 degrees. I was told they had to do it, to get the temperature down before it caused brain damage. Too, I needed more surgery, and they couldn't do it until the fever was under control.

I don't know what happened after that. I don't remember the ice being removed, or the fans turned off, or going into surgery. I just remember waking up, and seeing my sweet doctor bending over me, crying. He said, "Oh, thank God, you're back! I thought I had lost you!" When I realized what he had said, I thought, "That's funny. I didn't see Jesus this time."

I learned then that I had undergone surgery again. This time, the cervix to my uterus was removed. That is the lower part of the upside-down, pear-shaped womb. My doctor told me that while I might get pregnant, I would never carry a fetus long enough to even know it was there. So I resigned myself to accept the fact that my family of three boys was all there ever would be.

I'm still hesitant to talk about the two separate 'near-death' experiences. They were nothing alike. The first time, when my twins were born, I knew I was about to die, but nobody else seemed to realize it. The vision of Christ was not an image of a man with a face, but the voice coming from the light was very real.

Other people have talked about being drawn to the light, and not wanting to come back. But I very definitely wanted to live. I begged God to let me live, and was granted my life, with the provision that I live it well.

The last time, I was the one who didn't know anything about being near death. I've never understood why the two experiences were so much different, unless God was not satisfied with the way I had lived in the meanwhile. Maybe, like Mr. Bradford had told me at school, "I'm tired of messing with you," maybe God was tired of messing with me.

I have never talked much about it before, and I will probably never talk about it again. But I cannot tell the story of my life without including the story of near-death. If anybody chooses to attribute it all to hallucination, so be it.

Chapter 18

CALIFORNIA

It has to have been during the short period when we were home in early 1957 that we bought our home in Iowa Park. It was one of the oldest houses in town, at the west edge. A few years previously, it had been a farm, outside of town. A developer had built a few houses around the area, so there were neighbors. We thought it would be a good place to settle down when we got ready to quit traveling with the pipeline. Until that time, we rented it to the people who were already living in it at the time.

Fuzzy memory again covers the time period of moving back to Humboldt. But we both vividly remember the cute little pink house we lived in while equipment was being prepared for the job in California. It had previously been a filling station, so it was just a three room 'shotgun' house. But we liked it.

The last time we were in Humboldt, for Ruth Vaughan's funeral, the little house was still there on the corner, close to downtown.

Again, I stayed in Humboldt while Bill helped with the equipment move. I have no memory of when we changed vehicles, or what it was, but I had a car then. After the men got established at the location, it was time for the women to go. A guy by the name of Max Kelly, a local Humboldt guy, had gone with the first group. He wanted his wife, Dixie, and their baby girl to come out, but she didn't have transportation. I had not met her before, but it was arranged that she and the baby would go with me and my three little boys.

Someplace in a chapter back there, when we just had Cecil, we had bought a two-wheel trailer, from Sears, to pull behind our vehicle, mainly so that we could take his crib and playpen, among other things people need when they just have one baby. Bill had built sideboards for it, with bows across to hold a tarp in place, making the trailer 'enclosed.'

Of course, the more kids we had, the less furniture we carried…. But the trailer was always loaded. We still have that David Bradley trailer, and the side-boards. We've been through a lot of vehicles, but that little trailer has remained in the family.

We left Humboldt, just as we always did, driving through: two young women and four children, pulling a trailer behind us. That maybe wasn't such a big deal, and nothing noteworthy happened, until we got to Lake Tahoe on the Fourth of July!!!!

We could not drive through town, due to the traffic. So, we parked and looked at the map. There was a little road that appeared to be a short cut to Marysville, California. So, we took it What we didn't know was that it was the scenic route through the High Sierra Mountains. By the time we realized where we were, there was no place to turn around.

Again, I will explain to you young people that highways then didn't necessarily mean "wide", or with guard rails along the outside of mountain roads. When it got dark, it was pitch black, and our headlights beamed into infinity. We couldn't stop, so I just kept inching on, feeling my way around hair-pin curves, but never meeting another car. Other people had better sense!!!!

Just about dawn, we reached the bottom, and Marysville, still all in one piece. I found a lighted corner, and stopped before I collapsed in fatigue.

Oh yes, it's easy to look back and laugh at some of the stupid things we did. But, after all, I was twenty-five years old, and in charge of the world! It really made me mad for Mama and Daddy to worry about me, for no reason. What could possibly happen?

At some point, we arrived in Fortuna, California. I got on my cell phone and called Bill on his…Okay, so I lie a little bit. Most likely, we drove around until we found something that looked familiar, like a company truck, or a pipe yard. Anyway, we found our men, and each went to our own temporary residence.

Our home turned out to be the downstairs apartment directly below one in which Dennis and his friend from college, Leonard

Price, were living. It was at the end of a street, with lots of room around it, so the little boys could play. They liked it there.

The house contained two more apartments, across from each of us, upstairs and downstairs. Across from me, there lived a young couple, just a few years older than Bill and me. I visited with the girl, but soon realized that she was alcoholic, and bad news.

Upstairs, across from Dennis, there was an oilfield crew, who were there on a temporary job, too. We saw them in passing, and spoke to them briefly. But the door to the boys' apartment was open to us quite often. We visited back and forth regularly, as other people with our gang were in and out.

The landlady was something else. I'm not sure what, but really something else!! I guess she was close to middle aged, single, and epileptic. It didn't take long to learn that she enjoyed her seizures in front of people, and could bring one on at will. She complained constantly, about anything she could think of, and was at my door at least once a day.

One such day, she stood in the doorway, listing all her gripes. I don't know where Bill was, but he should have been there. In the midst of a long dialog, she added, "And, besides, the men upstairs are tired of you bothering them!"

I asked, "Do you mean Dennis and Leonard complained?"

"Oh no," she said, "But the men in the other apartment did."

Very angry, I shot up the stairs to the oilfield workers' apartment, and knocked on their door. When one of them came to the door, I asked, "Have any of you guys complained to the landlady that I have been bothering you?"

One of them said, "Hell, NO! You could bother me all you wanted to, and I wouldn't complain!" The other men all laughed. I didn't see the humor at the time, nor did I appreciate the 'compliment'.

The woman had followed me up the stairs, and continued to agitate me. I saw Dennis's door open just a crack, and several sets of little eyes were lined up, looking out to see what was going on. It took a while for that to be funny, too.

Finally, I had enough when she began to taunt me with, "You want to hit me, don't you? Go ahead. Hit me. Hit me!!!" In my anger, I slapped the fire out of her, something I would be arrested for today.

She cried, "OUCH! That HURT!"

I said, "Well, dammit, I meant for it to hurt!"

Need I add, that is one of Dennis's favorite stories, to this very day? When I asked him to help me remember exactly what happened, he told me,

"When you caught her in the lie, she began to snarl and growl at you. You slapped the s*** out of her!"

Okay, so I just thought it was fire….

Dennis added, "And those weren't just little eyes staring at you. There was one BIG pair!"

Too soon, school started, and the boys went back to Kansas. Dennis was going back to a girl named Jody. He just wouldn't listen to his older friend, who told him to not get serious at his young age…..

Jody never forgave me for that, either!

School also started for Cecil. Since his birthday is in October, he couldn't go the previous year. He was almost 7, very smart, and knew such things as the alphabet, numbers, simple arithmetic, and a little bit of reading. So, after a couple of weeks without him bringing home any evidence of learning, I went to the school to see what was wrong. I was told "We don't expect anything from students the first year, except how to get along with other children!"

To say I was shocked is an understatement. I told the teacher that he had already had six years of training in that department!

I wasn't a very popular parent…..

Either the job moved, or we moved to a location closer to the yard. Anyway, our next house was in Rio Dell, just about 10 miles south of Fortuna. Speedy and Bill's brother, Buddy, had been on a job in Washington while we were in Fortuna.

But they joined us soon after the move out to Rio Dell. We had a nice Christmas there, before that job also ended. Speedy decided to go to Mississippi, where he had inherited part of his daddy's land. Buddy stayed with us, as we moved on to a tiny suburb of San Francisco, named El Cerrito. I don't remember why we were there, but the job didn't last long.

A year had passed since we bought that house in Iowa Park. We sent word home that we would need it soon, and for the renters to move out. Then, we headed home.

...living without Daddy...

Chapter 19

OUR OWN HOME

We got moved into our house, by gathering furniture that we had acquired through the years, and left with one or the other set of parents, borrowing other things, and buying only the bare essentials to set up permanent housekeeping.

A few days after we had settled in, Jimmy came running into the house, and said, "Mama, I can't find the landlord."

It was then that I realized that, all those years, the first thing we had told the little boys was that "Mr.[or Mrs.] So& So" was the landlord, [or landlady] and they must obey them. Every place we lived had rules that the children must learn, about what not to touch, and where they could play, among other things. Most of the time, they were not allowed to make too much noise, because the landlord might get upset.

When I told my little Jimmy, "Honey, we don't have a landlord, here. This is our own house," it took him a little while to understand. Finally, I told him "Daddy is the landlord!" That was all he needed. He ran around the yard, singing and hollering at the top of his voice. He certainly wasn't afraid of the landlord!

Shortly, a visit to Dr. Clark confirmed what I had suspected: Against all odds, I was pregnant, and had carried the baby long enough to be certain. Having made it that far, Dr. Clark said he felt there was a good chance that I could carry him almost full term. Since the muscles that deliver babies are in the cervix, and I no longer had that portion of my womb, this time I would need to have a caesarian section. But otherwise, he saw no problems.

Almost immediately, Bill got a call to go to Germany. It was a new kind of life for me and the little boys, living without Daddy at home, for a long period of time. It was just the first of many times that I would be totally responsible for them.

Cecil enrolled in school at home. He was so far behind his class that it caused him to feel inferior. We worked long hours at home, trying to catch him up with the children who were already spelling and adding two columns. I wished the California school system could see what it had done.

The little boy from next door discovered my three boys, and came over to play with them. He had a little sister that had to stay at home with a sitter. His daddy worked for the telephone company, and his mama was a nurse. The little boy's name was Mike. That's all I knew for a while.

I don't remember how I got acquainted with his parents. But I learned that Mike's last name was Leath. His little sister was Annette. His mama was Pat. And his daddy was Preston, that boy who had come with his parents to sees my family at Clara!

The reunion between Preston and me was just the beginning of friendship that really has to be considered family.

Preston's daddy had died some years before, but his mother was living at Valley View. He told her that he had found the Chambers, who were living down on Cash street, in Iowa Park. So, she began visiting Mama and Daddy. There could be a book written about their friendship, which began in 1920. And now their children had become friends. and their grandchildren, as well!

Pat and I also liked each other She was Dr. Clark's nurse, so I saw her during visits to him, more than at home.

I don't know why July 11 was set for the birth of my little girl, who was going to be named Hope Elaine. Dr. Clark didn't do the actual surgery, and I've forgotten that doctor's name. But maybe they set it for Friday, so that both of them could skip out on the weekend! Or maybe it was so that their offices would be closed, and it would be easier to look in on me. Sure....

I was wheeled into surgery, and came back out with.......
surprise......A BOY!!!!! One look at him and I certainly didn't
care! Good thing we had not named any of our boys Junior,
because that allowed our last one to be named after Bill. And, of
course, I chose to name him Clark, after the doctor who had cared
for me so carefully.

Billy Clark joined the family July 11, 1958.

Dr. Clark told me he was going on vacation, and when it was
time for the stitches to be removed, Pat would do it. He just forgot
to tell Pat!

I had complained that while I was in the hospital, I couldn't
get an aspirin, because it had not been ordered by the doctor. So,
when I called her to remove my stitches, she quipped "Sorry! I
can't do that. I don't have Doctor's orders!"

Of course, she broke all the rules of nursing, and performed that
operation without doctor's orders! Thank God! I didn't want to
leave them in another two weeks!

Little Grandma came to stay with us, after Billy was born. She
was a God-send. Not only did she help me, but the boys idolized
her. She would get on the floor and play with them, and tell them
stories all day long.

One day, while I was napping, Grandma decided she would
wash some clothes in my new automatic washer that hooked up
to the kitchen sink. She didn't know the secret of connecting
it, and didn't want to wake me. She tugged and pulled, and
pushed, but couldn't get it on. Not to be defeated, that spunky
little woman finally climbed up onto the cabinet, with the washer
hose in her hands, and pulled upward to the faucet.....

I woke up to the sound of a water fountain, and Little
Grandma screaming "Help! Help!" I ran for the kitchen, and
collapsed laughing in the dining room floor. Little Grandma was
still squatting over the sink with the faucet in her hands!

When plumber Bud Britt became a little too rough on her, I
had to remind him of a time years ago, when brother Buddy had

installed a bathroom with a commode by the back door of the Gilmore house. The first time Little Grandpa used it, he was so impressed that he flushed it several times while sitting down. He suddenly jumped up screaming….Bud Britt had hooked the commode up to the hot water tank!

Time passed slowly, but eventually Bill did come home, some time in September. During that time, he and Preston met. Preston later said that Bill had gone over and offered to help him with a chore. From that meeting, they became the best of friends.

Bill also renewed an old friendship with Bud Thompson, and his wife, Billie. I didn't know either of them very well at the time.

Mother and Daddy's 50th Wedding Anniversary was Jan. 29th, 1959. I was living at home, but since I was the youngest child, it never occurred to me that it was MY responsibility to plan a reception. None of my siblings mentioned it to me, and I never even thought of it.

Sometime around the middle of January, Marvel called and asked me what I had planned. It took me by surprise, and I told her I had not made plans. She hung up quickly, and that was that.

I was 27 years old at the time, and not very wise in social ways. Not only that, but I had three small boys and a baby. If anybody had suggested I make arrangements, I would have tried. I just didn't know I was supposed to.

My siblings got together and made plans to come home on the previous weekend. They just didn't bother to include me. I heard about it after it was over. My little boys just happened to go down to visit that day. Whether the slight was intended or not, it hurt.

Bill stayed home a short time before he went to Venezuela in early 1959. There he worked on a barge, laying pipe in Lake Maraciabo . He was gone for a few months, again.

When he came home that time, he brought me a pair of midget parrots, better known as "Love Birds." I named them Maggie and Jiggs. They talked when he got them. But they only spoke Portuguese......

I see that I failed to note the birth of nephew Cary Glasgow in February, 1957. Two years later to the month, Veneta contributed the final player to our ball team, with the birth of Little Grandma's seventh grandson, Clay.

The reason the births of my own sibling's offspring have not been recorded in my saga is simply because they lived elsewhere, and were not involved in our daily lives at home. And, let's face it: I don't remember when any of them were born! But they are all pretty special to me!

...that winter in Minnesota...

Chapter 20

WAY UP NORTH

When Bill returned from South America, he went to work on the construction of the new runway at Sheppard AFB, that was being built to accommodate B52 Strato-fortresses that were coming in 1960.

It was on that job that he worked for a man named T.T. Miller. Mr. Miller had a teen-aged son named Mitch. Yep! That's him!

That's where Bill was working in May of 1959, when he was called to go to Grand Forks, North Dakota.

A man by the name of Carl Wilbanks, who he met on the runway job, wanted to go with him. Brother Bud also went. They left ahead of me, as usual. I don't remember Carl's wife's name, but she drove her car along with me and the boys.

I have one reason to remember that trip vividly: I had stopped to change Billy's diaper, and got pretty far behind the other woman. So, I was speeding down the highway at 80+ mph, when my front passenger tire blew out! Don't ask me how I knew how to control the car. I just threw my body on the steering wheel, held on and rode it out. I'm very sure there was an Angel with me. But I had to change the tire alone!

We had a nice place to live in Grand Forks, and we had a lot of fun with the new couple, as well as those from previous jobs. Dennis had married Jody by then, and left her at home, pregnant.

Buddy and Dennis found a skating rink, and began to spend all their spare time there. Once in a while, we would go to the rink, too. Carl and his wife loved to keep our kids, and we appreciated the chances to get out.

Dennis reminded me to tell about a guy named Ballinger, from Humboldt. Whatever his first name, Ballinger was a genius, and had designed a machine for Peewee, that made part of the work a lot easier and faster. But he was also an idiot!

He had an eye for the ladies, and me in particular! And he was always at the rink. As I was putting my skates on, invariably I'd look up, and Ballinger would be sitting on his haunches in front of me, grinning and drooling...Literally! If I was nice to him, it made him worse. It wasn't my nature to be rude to anybody, but in his case, I made an exception! Neither Bill nor Dennis nor Bud would try to divert him, as they just thought it was funny.

Bud met a girl named Geraldine, better known as Jerry, at the skating rink. He didn't bring her home to meet me, though....

The pipe yard was located on the Air Force Base outside Grand Forks. I quite often took lunch to the guys. One day, I was waiting for them to shut down to eat, when I saw the dope pot catch fire, and a man running from it, with his clothes burning. It was Buddy!

Everything happened so fast, I can't remember how he was put into my car. I drove as fast as that vehicle could travel, about 12 miles into town, to the hospital. Buddy was severely burned over his body and face, and screaming in agony. He was totally unaware that I was driving the car, or even where he was. I had never before seen anybody in that much pain.

I don't know why Jerry and I didn't run into each other at the hospital. I guess I was there while she was at work, and she was there when I was home with my kids. Bud spent quite a long time recovering, with life-time scars.

It was getting close to time for school to start, and I didn't want more problems with the boys learning. So, I decided to go home. Carl's wife wanted to drive along with me, until she would turn west, toward Woodward, Oklahoma.

Right after I got home, and saw everybody, I started crying. Daddy told me I needed to go back. I just thought it would be a mistake, for the boys. So I went to see Miss Kidwell. She said, "Maryanne, it doesn't matter if a kid loses a year in school.

But it does matter if he loses time with his daddy. You go back to Bill." And so, I turned around and drove straight back to Grand Forks. I got there just in time to move again.

As soon as Carl's wife left, he went on a drinking binge. Bill had to put him on a bus to Woodward. By that time, we had been told a story that made our hair stand on end: Carl had been in a mental institution for the criminally insane. The woman was working there when they met. When he was released, they got married. He was there for killing his father with an ice pick. The woman must have been crazy, too.

Those were the people who were keeping our children when we went out! You just never know who you are trusting.

We arrived in Forest Lake, Minnesota just in time to enroll Cecil and Jimmy in school. It was Jimmy's first year.

We found a cute little cottage, right on the lake. We even had a boat dock, just no boat! It was available because of the time of year. It was a popular meeting place for our people, and we really enjoyed it.

That's when I finally met Jody, the girl Dennis had moaned over in California! And I also met Denise, that sweet little baby girl.

Oh, yes! One day, Buddy asked me to go to the train station to pick up that girl from North Dakota. She was coming for a visit. So, I also met Jerry for the first time.

The job at Forest Lake was different than any the men had ever been on before. The pipe was being strung across a lake, and they used a helicopter to set river weights along it. All the men had a ball, and even my little Cecil got to go for a ride in it. They just didn't invite the women!

We were just north of Minneapolis and St. Paul. One day, just driving around in St. Paul, we passed a car lot. And on that lot was a bright red Oldsmobile station wagon! It had our name on it.... after all, we needed space for four kids. And it was RED!

What more did we need to prove it was meant for us? So, we traded in the nice Buick we were driving at the time. We drove that station wagon off that lot!

Three days later, at the grocery store, I misjudged the distance to a pole behind me. I forgot the station wagon was a lot longer than a car. So, we took it back to get the bumper and back fender fixed.

When it was ready, we went after it. On the way back to Forest Lake, we stopped behind a school bus, unloading kids. The car behind us didn't stop! He rammed us almost into the bus.

The next day, I went into town to tend to the insurance. After I left that office, I drove to a motel where Jo and Clifford Hunt were living. I had left my glasses there a couple of days before. I parked four feet from the front door, and left the motor running. The three older boys were in the very back end. Billy was in the front seat with me.

Jo opened the door, and handed me my glasses. Suddenly, the station wagon took off in reverse, full speed, in a half circle. It stopped when it hit a delivery truck across the parking lot. Thank God, the kids were not hurt. But the vehicle......the back end was smashed up nearly to the seat. How on earth it kept from killing the little boys!

There was no doubt that Billy had pulled the gear shift down, then fell into the floor onto the accelerator. Believe me, I never left a car running, with children in it, again !

We tried, to no avail, to get our old car back. But we were stuck with Jinx. And after she was fixed that time, she became a beloved part of the family.

Winter set in. Our lake froze solidly, and the local residents began driving their cars across it, rather than going around the roads. Bill chipped ice out for his tea. And the little boys skated to their hearts content, without skates!

A snow storm hit one day while the little boys were at school. They caught the bus about 200 feet from the house. But that day, the snow drifts settled around the house, up to the windows.

When it was time for the bus to bring them home, the snow plow had cleared the road, but that added to the amount that had to be forged from there to the house. I bundled up, and tried to make a path before they got home. But the bus was early, and I hadn't finished. I had to push through the snow up to my waist, to reach them. I carried Jimmy, and Cecil walked behind me, with his head barely above the snow.

It was 40 below that winter in Minnesota, and the frost line was 30 inches into the ground. But it wasn't as cold feeling as it had been in Rock Springs, Wyoming, at 20 below and the wind blowing.

...it was just the birds...

Chapter 21

WAY DOWN SOUTH

The job was finally finished, and we headed south, for Bill to run a job for Irish Pipe Coating, where Louie Cowsar was in charge. Our regular gang returned to Kansas for the rest of the winter.

Our next location was in Liberty, Texas. We left that ice and snow behind, and arrived in Liberty on a warm November day. When I took the little boys to school, there were children arriving bare-foot, and in short pants!

That sun didn't last long, and rains set in. That's all that Bill remembers about Liberty, having to wade through knee-deep mud. We weren't there long before he called Dennis to come down and take over the dope machine.

We lived in another motel where other workers, including Dennis, were staying. There were some brothers from Arkansas that we had not previously met. One was very intelligent appearing. The other was a bit of a hillbilly, to say the least! We have always remembered him for a couple of expressions he used. For example, to him, I was "Mrs. Bill". When he wanted something, he would say, "Lordy, Mrs. Bill, would it be ill mannered if I asked for a glass of water?" That became a standard line, repeated by others for years to come.

Dick and Ann lived at Lake Charles at the time. They came to spend a weekend with us. I don't remember where we kept the bird cage in Grand Forks or Forest Lake, but in Liberty, there was no place for it, except on a chest in the bathroom. One evening, Ann was taking a bath. Suddenly, she was out of there, with her face bright red. I had forgotten that Maggie and Jiggs knew how to 'wolf whistle". Ann swore that somebody was watching her take her bath, and whistled at her! We never convinced her it was just the birds!

Because of the lack of space, we put the bird seed in the bathtub, to keep it from scattering around the bathroom. It was a fatal mistake. Somebody left the commode lid open, and Maggie tried to fly over it. With her clipped wings, she couldn't make it. I found her drowned body in the commode.

After that, Jiggs would not stay in the cage with the door open. He followed me everywhere, wanting on my shoulder. A few months later, at home, I stepped backwards, not knowing he was there. And I killed my precious bird.

A couple of years later, Dennis found another midget parrot, and got him for us. His name was Jose, and we had him for many years.

We ended the decade of the 1950's at Liberty. And that's where I will end this part of my book.

End of Book II

BOOK III

Table of Contents
Book III

Racing Along Life's Highway

Chapter:

...loving that old house...

Chapter 1

WELCOME HOME

The decade of the sixties began with us at Liberty, Texas. When the job was over, we went back home for a while. Bill went to work out on the construction of the new US 287 Freeway that would by-pass Iowa Park and Electra, and Vernon.

We all began settling in again, loving that old house that belonged just to us. Pat and Preston had moved by then to their home on Aldine. I had not met the new neighbors. But that would soon change....

The old house was odd shaped, with the living room extending in front of the bedrooms, small dining room and kitchen. It had a porch that wrapped around the front, and the east side. The steps outside were located on the west end of the front part of the porch. The entry door was around the porch, and entered the living room from the east porch. The kitchen and dining room connected to the end wall of that porch, so for a person to come in, and get to the kitchen from the front, he would have to walk around the porch, into the living room, turn into the center bedroom, turn back to the east, through the dining room door. Turning again, he would be looking toward the back wall of the kitchen, where the sink was located, with a small window above it. The back door opened inward on the east wall of the tiny kitchen. It was a maze to anyone not familiar with the layout.

Bill was at work, Cecil and Jimmy were at school, and Kenny was outside playing. I was in the kitchen, washing dishes, when suddenly a man screamed behind me. I turned around in terror, and saw that it was Carl. His face was flushed and his eyes were blazing. He broke into a run for those few feet. I just froze, not knowing what was going to happen. I couldn't get out the back door. Then, just inches from me, he stopped. His expression changed, and he started to moan and cry. He put his arms around me, and cried on my shoulder. I didn't know what to do.

It seemed like an eternity, but his wife came in behind him. She motioned to me to be quiet. Then she began talking to him calmly, and got him to turn loose of me. She got him out of the kitchen, into the dining room, and sat down at the table.

I sat at the table with the two of them, and listened to Carl cursing Bill, because he had fired him, and sent him home. He kept asking me where Bill was, that he was going to kill him. His wife motioned again for me to be quiet. I told Carl that I didn't know where Bill was, that he was out in the oilfield somewhere.

Eventually, the woman got Carl to leave, still threatening to kill Bill. When I saw that they had left my driveway, I ran next door, to borrow the phone, since ours was not yet connected. The man answered the door, and let me in. I called Henry Jones, and told him what had happened. Henry was still the Constable in Iowa Park, before the town had a police force.

Henry told me I needed to keep a gun in the house. I answered that Bill would not let me have a gun. Henry said, "Well, as much as you are alone, he had better let you have a gun." He told me to have the neighbor to watch the house, and call him if the car returned.

What a welcome home!

When I hung up, I introduced myself to Roy and Janette Perry. Roy's sister, Betty, had been a classmate of ours. They had moved back home, after living elsewhere for a number of years. They had three children. The oldest girl, Darlene, was in high school. Dale was just a little older than Cecil. And there was a little girl about a year younger than Kenny, by the name of Linda.

The kids all grew up with my boys, and left home at the same times. Roy died several years ago. After a couple of divorces, and raising her own four boys, Darlene moved back home with her mother. They are still next door, when I venture home....

Chapter 2

MONTANA / NORTH DAKOTA

In the early spring of 1960, Bill got a call to go to Baker, Montana. The timing was just right to convince Little Grandma to go with us. It was the only long trip she ever made in her lifetime, and she did keep a journal. Unfortunately, we don't know where it went, after she died. I could surely use that help, now.

I should be able to recall more about Baker than just that we really enjoyed the time we spent there. I do know that Buddy and Jerry got married while we were there, and my Mama stood in for both of theirs!

We had a nice house, and the city had a small swimming pool nearby. I took the kids there a lot. And outside of town, there was a rocky area that we all went to frequently. The boys loved to climb over them, while the rest of us found a spot to sit and watch.

That was the first job that A.W, and Billie Faye Smith were on. They had just adopted their baby grandson, Richard. Billie Faye was a good mother. Nobody could argue with that. Her problem was that she was alcoholic and a drug addict. When she was sober, she was the most wonderful friend a person could have. She just could not stay sober.

I give her credit for taking care of Richard, even when she was drunk. Often, she would be arrested for public drunkenness. Each time, she would ask the police to call me to pick up the baby. She trusted me with him, and I had him often enough to grow attached. At the time, Billy was getting close to 2 years old, and I could have added Richard without any problem. But A.W. and Billie Faye were friends. Bill and I couldn't betray that, by trying to get him.

Dennis and Jody were on that job, too, with little Denise. When the job was over, Jody went back to Humboldt to have her second boy, Dennis Dean. Most of us moved to Mandan, North Dakota. Dennis went to another job in Colorado.

Our abode in Mandan was another of those memorable living arrangements. It was supposed to be a motel unit. But it was actually something like an old trailer with bunk beds built along one wall, and enough space to walk by them from one end to the other.... a very short distance, to more beds! Three kids and three adults in a space not big enough to cuss a cat... We all learned to love the outdoors!

Fortunately, the job was shorter than our endurance. In my mind, we moved back to Baker before going on to Laurel, Montana. Maybe I'm wrong. Nobody can remember, for sure.

I have no memory of Laurel, not even the place we lived. No doubt it was another motel, since it was a temporary location. But Dennis was there, and he does have a good memory! Most especially, he remembers Bill being with him, when they went to a drive-in for a bite to eat. The bill came to less than $5. Bill handed the car-hop a twenty....Dennis told her "Keep the change!", and quickly drove off!

Yeah, that was a typical Dennis stunt....and I can still hear him laughing as Bill fumed!

Laurel is near Billings, just about 50 miles north of Powell, Wyoming, where Lillie still lives. It was just natural that we would go through there on our way back home.

Lillie had recently married Bob Barber. His wife, Ruth, had been Lillie's best friend all through their years in Wyoming. They had three children, but the older girl and boy both left home before our visit. Bob's daughter, Colleen, was near Berry Lee's age. Dorothy was just Cecil's age. Joetta was still in college at Laramie.

Little Grandma wanted to see Yellowstone, and of course, the rest of us had never tired of the park. Lillie's family also wanted to join us, so we all drove over, in separate cars. We camped in Lillie's tents at Lower Falls, and made that famous 8 shaped route around the park. Then, we left through the south gate, as Lillie and Bob returned to her home.

Again, I need Little Grandma's journal. I don't recall the trip home, but all I know is, when she was along, there was never a dull moment.... She brought a lot of joy to all our lives.

...another Billy Joe Gilmore...

Chapter 3

RIFLE, COLORADO

Summer was gone when we went to Rifle. It was time to enroll Cecil and Jimmy in school again.

That was another of those places that we will never forget. Lots of our friends were there, including Smitty and Billie Faye. Most of us lived in one Motel, where the individual units wrapped around a common yard. I don't remember where the Smiths lived, though.

Jody had just had Dennis Dean. She came out about the first of October, when he was 9 days old. She and Dennis lived across the yard from us.

Next door to us was Charlie Hunt, Clifford's brother. I forgot in previous chapters to mention that they were the sons of Jim Hunt, the man Bill was with when the train hit them in Medicine Lodge, Kansas.

Charlie's wife was Kay, and that was the first time I met her. She was a real character....a ding-bat....kind of pathetic, but likeable. She had a crush on Bill, and made no secret of it ! We all laughed about it, but we never knew what to do about it. It didn't bother Charlie.

One day, she was sitting in my house when Bill came by to get something. When he left, he kissed me. Kay said, "Well, I want a kiss, too!" So he walked over and gave her a kiss on the cheek. "NO!" She pointed at me and said. "You kiss me the way you kissed HER!"..... So... he did.....

The Yockey brothers, Dick and Chuck were there, too.. Chuck was a musician deluxe....Later, when Roy Clark became famous, we didn't think that Chuck looked like him... but Roy Clark looked just like Chuck Yockey, and acted like him, too! In fact, I think he stole his act from Chuck.

Harry and Betty Carey, and their huge family were there. Harry was the third brother of Ruth's, so the entire family worked with her and Peewee at different times. Betty was known as the most congenial woman alive. No matter how tiresome things got, Betty always had a big belly laugh.

Once again, the entire gang got together for picnics in a huge park. With my four kids, Betty's seven, Jody's two, and Jenny's three, it was quite a sight. They all got along well....even Harry Dean!

Ruth and Peewee had adopted Donnie and Debbie by then, but they and Daryll stayed in Humboldt during the school year, just as Dennis had, as a child. Somewhere along the line, they had changed the name of the company from Western Pipe Coating to 3-D Pipe Coating, for Dennis, Daryll and Donnie. They didn't have Debbie at that time, or it would have been 4-D!!!

We had heard about another Billy Joe Gilmore on the pipeline, all those years... and his brother, James.... We really thought people were just telling us that... But at Rifle, the other one was on that job, for another contractor, doing another part of the process. His wife's name was Mary!!! We all got our mail by General Delivery.... When one of us went to the post office, we had to go through the mail and decide which was ours! It was quite a deal....but we never met the couple, face to face.

Some of our gang kept the bars in business. Bill and I seldom ever went to one. But one Saturday night, we joined the Hunts and Yockey brothers, and some others. We got tired before the rest of them, and left.

The next morning, we heard that a fight broke out, and most of them were involved. It was a matter that required the police.

Anyway, we were at Ruth and Peewee's house, discussing how lucky we were that we had left early. Ruth had a worried look on her face. Peewee was glaring at both of us. Then he got up, walked over to my chair and stood over me, with his finger shaking in my face. "Young lady," he yelled, "You don't belong in places like that. I don't ever want to hear of you being in another one! Then you won't have to worry about leaving before a fight starts!"

He turned on his heel and marched back to his chair and plopped down, and glared at me some more. I felt like my daddy had spanked me! But I was glad that he cared enough to scold me.

The job ended on Kenny's 6th birthday, December 15th. It was the last time Bill would work for Peewee. 3-D Pipe Coating was dissolved soon afterward. But we all remained close friends for the rest of Ruth's and Peewee's lives.

Bill and I had both a car and a pickup at Rifle. When we started home, he insisted that we take one of the 'short cuts' like the one Dixie and I took in California....I begged and cried, but no way was he going to drive all the way to Denver, when that road cut through to Colorado Springs!

First, driving the pickup, he took off and left me, as the car slipped all over the road. Then he stopped and bawled me out for not keeping up with him. I tried to tell him I was driving as fast as I could.

Finally, he said "You drive the pick up, and I'll drive the car!" So, I got in the pickup, with it's snow tires....and took off. After a while, I stopped and waited for him. Then he bawled me out for running off and leaving him!

So, I told him to get in front of me, and lead the way....he did.... and drove off into a snow filled ditch...... We sat there for a couple of hours, wondering if we were going to die there, because there was no traffic on the road. Finally, a snow plow came by, and pulled him out.... and, with a clear road ahead, we made it across.... and all the way home.

...square nails and all...

Chapter 4

ESTABLISHING ROOTS

The following year is really fuzzy to me. I know that we got Cecil and Jimmy back into school at Iowa Park. And that has to have been when I started working in the Primary Sunday School Department at First Baptist. Both Jimmy and Kenny were in that department while I was teaching, and that would be the right age.

I met one of the best friends I ever had through that job. Betty and Jim Coleman had one little boy, Brett, and a little girl, Becky, in the department. Their older boy, Billy, was about Cecil's age, and was in the next age group. They had just moved to town, and Betty and I hit it off immediately.

Betty was the most interesting woman I had ever known. I don't know what her I.Q was, but she was so intelligent that I felt dumb! When I would go to visit her, she would be reading an encyclopedia for entertainment. Jim was smart, but he lagged behind her. Nevertheless, the conversations were stimulating.

Both had a sense of humor as well. It's a good thing, because Betty was not your typical domestic housewife. She dressed like a farmer, and actually did outside chores. She wore no make-up, and had a long braid down to her hips. She raised chickens, and took the eggs to town to sell. She was one of a kind, and everybody soon knew who she was.

Billie Thompson had grown up mostly in an exclusive section of North Dallas....and if I have my facts straight, Betty lived nearby, during their teen years. So, they already knew each other before Betty moved to Iowa Park. At the time, I still didn't know Billie all that well....but I was told a funny story about an incident in our local variety store.

One day, Betty was in front of Billie at the check-out counter. As Betty left the store, the clerk turned to Billie and said, "Betty is so sweet. But somebody should tell her that you just don't go to town dressed like that..."

Billie replied, "Well, I guess if you were born with a silver spoon in your mouth, you wouldn't care what people thought, either!"

The report was that the woman almost fainted ! Since she was a royal snob that we all disliked, I would have given my eye teeth to have been present for that put-down!

Bill was working for Peewee Morton, and welding for the public on his own as well, during this time. Little Billy wanted to go with him on one job, which was for an oil company. When he got sleepy, Bill put him in the pickup for a nap.

Later, Bill said something told him to go look at Billy.... but he was gone! He saw something moving in the slush pit full of old oil. He ran as fast as he could, and caught hold of our baby, who had been scratching the sides of the pit, trying to hang onto a little limb, but still kept slipping again.

Bill brought that child home, and we both cried with him. We came so close to losing him.

Sheppard Air Force Base began a major update, and was selling the old frame barracks, and installing new brick buildings in their place. The price was right, so Billy Joe and Buddy both bought one. Buddy had his set beside their mother's house. And ours was set beside that farm house, as we soon learned it just was not big enough for our family.

I can't remember the exact time frame, but eventually we had the barracks remodeled into our present home.... well, actually just the center part. In the beginning, we had a beautiful linoleum with flecks of gold embedded into the various colors that covered a beige background. The living room was beige, the kitchen was turquoise. The boys had two rooms between the four of them, and sometimes changed rooms. One was painted federal blue, with a white ceiling. The other was fire-engine red, with a yellow ceiling. My room was originally white, with black trim, and a red bed spread. We made up for all those years when we had no choice about the colors of the houses we lived in. And we loved every room.

We worked on it in stages, as we had the money. We had borrowed $1200 for the building and moving costs, and just decided we wouldn't go any deeper into debt for the construction. But we did keep a record of our expenditures. When we were finished, our home had cost us $3000.

Shortly after moving into our new house, Billy disappeared from home. We were frantically searching for him, and had neighbors joining in the hunt. I will never know what made me finally go into the house, down the hall and open the door to that little linen closet. There, I found my little boy, crumpled on the floor, crying in a very weak voice, "Mama, please let me out!" Even after I had him in my arms, that little cry just kept saying those words over and over. I knew he had suffered another terrible trauma.

I have never known how he got in there, and pulled the door to behind him. It doesn't have a knob on the inside. But if one of the other boys had put him in there, they would have remembered when we started searching for him. Thank God, I found him.

Later, we tore the old farm house down.... square nails and all.... At the time, we had no thought of it's being a landmark for Iowa Park, but it was. We have been told that our well supplied part of the town with water in the early days. But 'progress' was underway!

A couple of years later, we extended the house to include the den, carport, and utility room. We bricked the outside at that time. It was many years later that we added on to our bedroom on the west end.

I joined the PTA, and we became members of the establishment! We had our own pew at church, and visited our parents often. We began to settle into living in Iowa Park.

...imagination worked overtime...

Chapter 5

NEW ORLEANS

Our newly established family routine at home was interrupted again in the spring of 1962, when Bill was called to a job in New Orleans, where Speedy was. I stayed home until the end of school, then the boys and I joined him.

We found a nice upstairs apartment with the stairway on the outside, which gave us total privacy from the family below. That isn't to say that they had privacy from us....I'm sure they learned new curse words from my four little boys' romping above them.

I don't remember their names, but the couple below was a pair of food addicts....Both weighed well over 300 pounds... maybe 500. The man was a chef. Obviously his wife liked his cooking! They were young enough to be the parents of a three year old little girl.

If we bothered them, then they paid us back, all in one night. We heard every curse word they knew! Such crashing occurred that we thought they must be killing each other. We decided against calling the police, when the noise stopped.

The next day, we learned that their bed had broken, sending them both to the floor. Considering that it was an ordinary, full size bed, with no special bracing for overweight people, we just wondered how it lasted as long as it did.... most especially, during romantic nights! Our imagination worked overtime on that one!

We lived just a few blocks from the Lake Ponchatrain beach, which had an amusement park attached. At the time, the city was segregated, and the beach was all White. It was beautiful, and a wonderful place to take the family. We went often.

I don't remember where the young girl lived that baby sat for us on a regular basis, but she became a friend. On one outing to the beach, she went with us. She and I were lying on our blanket, while Bill took all the boys into the water.

Suddenly, we realized that some young guys had decided to make a move on us. We looked at each other, and grinned. Then, when the two of them plopped down on our blanket, we both began to laugh. One of them asked, "What's so funny?"

The girl answered, "Oh, we were just wondering what you are going to do when her husband and four kids come out of the water..."

The boys both laughed and said, "Oh, S u r e........"

Just then, here came Bill, Cecil, Jimmy, Kenny and Billy...... You never saw two young men move so fast!!!!

During segregation, the black people had a beach farther down the lake side. The last time I was in New Orleans, the white beach had been completely taken over, and had become a trashy, dirty place. After seeing the results of Hurricane Katrina in 2005, we know why.

Before Bill had gone to New Orleans, he had promised me that he would wait until I got there before going to the French Quarter. But of course, he didn't. So, he had no interest in going back... at least, with me! He tried to placate me with driving through, with the kids in the car....

Well, it took me another 20 years, but I finally got to go to the French Quarter..... But that's another story for another chapter!

Smitty and Billie Faye Smith were also on that job. It was there that I was called to pick little Richard up at the police station for the last time. Smitty came after him when he got off from work. I was tempted again to try to take the child away from them. But again, I left it alone.

We got word that Bill's only niece, Jamie Lynn was born to Buddy and Jerry that summer. It was a while before we got to see her.

We really loved New Orleans, and I'm glad we lived there while it was still a beautiful, clean city. And the French Quarter's raciest shows were all girls in scanty costumes.....instead of being the sleezy gay spots we found in later years

The job moved to New Iberia, then on to Jennings, Louisiana. The summer was ending, and school was about to start. So, I left Bill there, and went home....for the last time. That was the end of my traveling to pipeline jobs.

...our old pew, second from the front...

Chapter 6

SHIFTING GEARS

A nother phase of life began that would be a series of changes over the next few years. When Bill came home from Louisiana, he built his welding shop in our back yard, and BILL GILMORE WELDING CO. was born. His first ad read "I can weld anything... including a broken heart." That's all it took for him to rake in the business from oil companies and local truckers. We set up the black desk in the den, and I kept books for him.

In January, 1963, Dennis went on a job to Das Island, in the Arabian Gulf. Danny Joe had been born the previous August. Jody didn't want to be alone with their three children while he was gone, so she came to stay with us for a couple of months. We enjoyed the time together. Our kids all got along well together. But then, they already thought we were all one big family, from being together so much on the pipeline. They just had to mind all the grownups!

We became very involved in church again. We bought bright red blazers for all four of the boys, and reserved our old pew....the second from the front, on the right side of the sanctuary.

Helen Miller came by one day and said, "Billy is sure going to be sick of that red blazer by the time he grows out of Cecil's!" Considering the 8 years between them, I guess Billy was relieved when the jackets were passed on to another family, rather than all being handed down to him!

Brother Thompson was the pastor, and also the RA Boys leader. Our older boys loved him, and RA became an important part of their lives.

I became the leader of the teen-aged girls group, those too old for GA's.... can't remember the name. Anyway, that was the first time that I felt like an intelligent woman. Those girls all loved me, and I loved them. There were confidences that I never broke, even though I had a lot of praying to do. I can see all the faces, and wish the names had not escaped me....When one of them sees me now, they always come to tell me hello, and give me a hug.

The boys became model car addicts. The local dime store was then TG&Y, and the manager soon learned that he could sell lots of model car kits by having contests on a regular basis. Cecil and Jimmy became skilled at customizing theirs, with fabric interiors and perfect paint jobs....I think they won 99% of the contests. Cecil has kept most of them over the years.

They all also began playing Little League Baseball. I sometimes had three games to attend in one evening, at three different fields. Once in a while, I had to make a choice of which to miss. I just had to take turns on which boy didn't have Mama in the stands.

During this time, I became re-acquainted with my old classmate Mary Coleman Catron. I had only seen her a couple of times in the years since her accident following our graduation from high school.

She had been living in a girls' boarding house on 9th street in Wichita Falls. There was a balcony from the second story over the front porch. She leaned over the railing to talk to a boy below. The railing broke, and she fell to the ground. Her back was broken, as well as other bones.

Her boyfriend told her it didn't matter, that he still wanted to get married. So, they married and had three children.

Because she was young, and inexperienced, she had signed a release that absolved the owner, a prominent doctor, from any future responsibility after the initial hospital bills were paid. Unfortunately, she had many internal injuries, and an infection in one of her legs that eventually required it to be removed.

Her husband just couldn't take it, and left her alone with the children. When I found her living in Iowa Park, she was in a wheel chair, living on welfare. If that had happened today, she would have been taken care of all her life.

We became very close. I also met her next-door neighbor, Nina Williams. The three of us enjoyed many cups of coffee over the next several years.

In January, 1964, I made up for failing to give Mama and Daddy a celebration on their Golden Anniversary. I decorated my home, and made all the plans for a big bash. All their friends, came. But there was a couple of strangers that also came by with a gift. Mr. and Mrs. Hayes, Pat Leath's mother and daddy, said they had heard so much about the Chambers that they felt like they were friends. Needless to say, they were from that day on!

...country bumpkins in the big city...

Chapter 7

VACATION TIME

I don't remember exactly when Bill went to Kharg Island and /or Saudi Arabia the first time, but it was sometime in early 1964. He left a hired man to take care of the welding shop. Once again, we had to learn to live without him at home. It wasn't easy. But I tried to corral four rowdy boys.

The New York World's Fair was going on during that year. Bill asked me to meet him in New York City when he returned from the job. Little Grandma again kept the boys, so that I could go. I don't remember the month, but it had to have been summer, because of the clothes we wore. That's one thing we do have pictures of, even though they are out of order in an album, just as all the rest of them!

I remember the fair pretty well, but not as clearly as some other incidents....attributed to the fact that we were country bumpkins in the big city. Whichever one of us that arrived first waited for the other at the airport....and I don't remember which way it was. But after we met, we went to a cab, and Bill gave them the name of the hotel he had stayed at on his stop there on the way overseas.

The cab driver drove us in circles, knowing we couldn't do anything about it. What should have been a 20 minute drive took an hour. The bill was horrendous.

Then, Bill forgot that the contractor from Saudi had met him in New York, and footed the bill for the hotel. We weren't prepared for that expense either. Don't remember the cost, but $50 a night would have been highway robbery then....Good thing Bill had kept a lot of cash for the trip, but I hated to spend it all on one night!

Finally, we went to dinner in the dining room....the same one where Bill had been asked to put on a tie before entering, on his first visit. [He got in by wearing his bolo tie....much to the amusement of his Arab boss.] Again, he had not noticed the manner in which the food was ordered....that is, each item had to be ordered separately. So, we each ordered a steak. When it came, that's what we had: a steak. No potato. No salad. We sat and ate them just as if we knew what we had done!

And he paid the humongous bill. Then we ate hot dogs the rest of the time!!!

Billy would be starting to school in the fall of 1964, and I was a room mother for the first time. It was much different then, when each room was free to do whatever they pleased for the various parties. We met in the spring to make plans for all of them.

At that planning meeting, I met another mother, by the name of Corliss Wallace. Her little boy would be in Billy's room when school started. We became friends, and as the weeks passed, the two families met. Her husband was Orville. They had a girl in Kenny's grade named Robyn. And the little boy was Matthew.

The family liked us so well that when their cocker spaniel got pregnant by a bird dog, they gave us a puppy out of the litter. Since Gomer Pyle was so popular on TV at the time, the boys promptly named him Gomer.

We had promised the boys a vacation when we got back home from New York City...We delivered, with a trip around the state of Texas. And what a trip it was! Of course, Gomer went with us.

Since the state is so large, we couldn't actually see it all in three weeks. But we tried! As we drove down Highway 287, the boys began a game of making jokes with the signs on the road. When we approached one that designated "climbing lane"... as they did then, for passing zones.... one of the boys said "Look at the lane climb!!!" When we went through the town of Antelope, there was a sign for the Baptist church. Jimmy said, "There's a church for Antelopes!"

Not to be outdone, when we passed through Bowie, little Billy asked, "Do you know where Bowie got it's name? Well, back in the olden days, women would walk down the streets. And men would jump out of doors and yell 'Boo!' Then the women would scream 'E e e e !' "

I must admit that from that day, Billy has been the family wit!

We drove down through Streetman and Winkler, where both Little Grandma's and Little Grandpa's relatives were. We visited with Aunt Myrtle, Rena Mae and N.D., and all the Neal's..... Jester and Gladene, and Alvin and Jetty.

I omitted an important story that should have gone in Book II. It has to be inserted here.....

When Bill and I married, the Gilmore family was all excited over Little Grandpa's nephews striking oil on their property. They were suddenly millionaires. So, I was anxious to meet them.

On our first trip down to Winkler, we had gone with Rena Mae and N.D. from Streetman, to see the Neals. [They were no kin. Just friends because of the family connection.] The talk was all about how much money they had.....When we reached the property line of their multi-acreage, we just kept driving. Eventually, we stopped at an old, run-down shack, with no windows. It had a TV antennae on the roof and a new car in the drive.

I thought we had stopped at the caretaker's home, and maybe he was going with us the rest of the way. But all of a sudden, everybody got out of the car.... I sat there alone until Bill turned around and told me, "We're HERE!" I almost died!

There were chickens in the house, and the only place to sit was an old car seat on one wall, and straight chairs around it... except for the new recliner that Jester sat in.

There were broom sticks nailed across the corners of the rooms, which served as closets for their clothes, just as I had known in my young childhood, before things changed!

We drove on to Alvin and Jettie's house. This one was tiny, but neat and clean, with new white paint. But there was no TV, or new car yet. Alvin had to get used to spending money, and he was very careful with it. They had no children.

Jester and Gladene had 4 children. [All four were raised as if they were poverty striken, all the time they lived at home.]

Well, on our vacation with the boys, we failed to show them all the oil wells on the Neal property. We had never told them this story. And nothing had changed from the scene I first saw, except that there were now screens on the windows and doors to keep the chickens out!

We cut over west from there, down to the center of the state, zig-zagging when necessary to see the Hill Country around Marble Falls, the capitol at Austin, and the Alamo at San Antonio. Then we went down to the coast of Corpus Christi.

From there, we drove on down to McAllen, to see more of Little Grandpa's nephews...the sons of his brother.

When we found Les Gilmore's home, it was a huge, beautiful brick house in a fine part of town. Les owned Gilmore Oil Company there. As we sat visiting, the boys were just enthralled with the house and everything in it. Then, the conversation turned to the Neals, who were also his cousins.

Les said, "If I had as much money as those guys, I would live like a king!" Our boys eyes got wide, and their mouths opened enough to swallow an orange.....

Once we were back in the car, the questions flew! It was very hard to convince them that those that lived so poorly had more money than the rest of us, all put together! And they never enjoyed it. What a shame.

Our vacation continued on, from McAllen to the south tip of Texas, back up the border to Laredo. We had done a lot of driving, and time was getting shorter. We had begun to drive after dark, when the boys were asleep.

Oh! Cecil did part of the driving, because he had his learners' permit...yes, at 14. There was a short period of time that kids could get their license at 15, and began their driver's training the school year prior to that birthday. It didn't last long, for some strange reason..... probably known as Cecil Gilmore...... Anyway, Jimmy had to wait 'til 16 for his!!

Again, I digress..... At Laredo, we stopped for gas. Some of the boys got out to use the bathroom. Bill and I stretched and changed drivers. Then we hit the road again.

Hours later, as the sun rose, the boys began to wake up. One of them asked, "Where's Gomer?" The screaming and crying began....but the boys were almost as loud as me!

Bill began cussing....but that car turned around right there in the middle of the road! And he was doing the driving....

Nine hours after we had left that station, we pulled back into it. There sat Gomer by the pump, just waiting for us to come back for him. He knew we loved him, and he never doubted us!

The rest of the trip was very happy, indeed. And Gomer didn't get out of the car without being seen, either!

We went on to Big Bend, to El Paso, then back through Odessa, to visit all the relatives there. Then, by mutual consent, we decided we didn't have time to go into the Panhandle part of the state. We were all ready to go home. We were tired, but it was a wonderful tired. It was also getting close to time for school to start.

It was Billy's first year to go to school. When report card time came around, he brought home a card full of "F's". I was beside myself. But Tommy was visiting at the time, and he thought it was really funny. He laughed and laughed. Then he told Billy, "That's all right. You are a well-adjusted boy!" And, he was....

...championship in a game of jacks...

Chapter 8

COASTING ALONG

The years kind of become one long one to me now. My life had not become calm, by any means. But it was a daily repeat of the day before: School, Church, Little League, visiting my Mom and Dad, and Little Grandma... We had a pool table in the den, and my house was full of boys every day after school.

The only difference was....was Bill overseas again? For how long this time?.....or was he at home?

As soon as he arrived home from each trip, he picked up where he had left off, in the shop in our back yard. Because he had so many jobs, he sometimes worked until 2 a.m. But of course, that didn't help, because people began to expect it of him, and his reputation was...take it to Bill Gilmore, and he will get it done, if it takes all night!!!

One of his biggest customers was a trucker by the name of Bobby Johnson. He had accumulated a few trucks, and was trying to keep them on the road. It was nothing unusual for Bill and me to be asleep in our bedroom, when we would hear a knock on our window at 3 or 4 a.m. if Bobby had a problem..... Since he worked around the clock, with little sleep, Bill had to, also.

He did a lot of oilfield welding, too. In 1965, a guy by the name of Bob Illingworth moved to Iowa Park, with Arcadia Oil Co. He and Bill liked each other right off. It wasn't long before Bill took me to meet Bob's wife, Bonnie, and their three kids....I can't remember their names....oh, yeah....they were Vickie, James and Cindy!

We became close to Bob and Bonnie, and the four of us went out at night a lot. Then, we would visit in the car for hours before somebody said, "I've got to go to bed!" We never ran out of things to talk about....at least, the men didn't, and Bonnie and I could always listen!

The real fun times came when we went to Lake Murray together, for a day of water skiing. Everybody else begged for their turn. I kind of gave up trying after nearly becoming a wishbone... At least, that chicken was dead when the bones were pulled apart!!

Then, there were those times when the Illingworth family would come to our house. Everybody played pool, but the kids got pushed out when Bill and Bob got serious...They had to wait for the table. So, they would pass the time on the floor, playing marbles, or jacks, or pick-up-sticks.

When the men discovered the kids were having too much fun, they would take the toys away from them, sit on the floor, and the competition began! Then, the kids could play pool....until midnight...or 1 a.m......or 2 a.m......Cindy would fall asleep on the floor....and soon James and Vickie were begging, "Daddy, let's go HOME!" But when the championship in a game of jacks is on the line, nothing else matters! Not even school the next day!!! Any kid should understand that!

It was just about that time that my boys all started working for Bobbie Johnson. He had acquired the local elevator by then. The kids mostly measured the moisture in the wheat, after it was loaded onto trucks. They were not in danger.

Bobby didn't pay them minimum wage, but at least he gave them a job, where they could earn their own money. They were proud of that, and liked having money in their pockets, and even buying some of their own school clothes. It was a good arrangement, for young kids. Actually, Kenny was only 11 at the beginning.

Later, we let him go stay with a couple in Fredrick who owned an elevator there. Of course, we knew them, and they were good people. He stayed nearly two weeks before I couldn't stand it any more.....But I was proud of all my boys.

Once Bill was home to stay, he joined the Volunteer Fire Department, and the Muleskinners. He was busy all the time.

We joined the square dance club, along with Pat and Oscar Singleton, and LaVern and Bill Harrington, and a lot of our other friends. It was fun, and Bill was extremely good at it. I've always been a little less coordinated when it comes to memorizing calls and steps. The boys often went with us, and sat on the sidelines, watching with the other kids.

Our friendship with Corliss created mixed emotions. All of us liked her, and I did enjoy our visits. However, there were times when we just wanted our family to be alone. She didn't understand that she was there too often, and too long. Moreover, she didn't realize how my mother resented her following me down to my folks house, and intruding on our time together. But she wanted to be a part of every aspect of our family.

We were in church for all the services during the week. When a new pastor came, we became close friends with Donald and Frances Wood, and went out with them often.

I took all the study courses that were offered, as well as a full class in Bible History. From teaching children, I moved up to teaching my own age class, then on to the more difficult challenge of the newly formed College and Career class. It required a lot of study and preparation, but I thrived on it.

...let's get on with it...

Chapter 9

MUDDY ROADS

This is that chapter I wish I didn't have to write. But there are some truths that cannot be denied. So, let's get on with it....

I was not a good mother. There were some years that Bill and I were not happy with each other. No matter how much we enjoyed time with our boys, no matter how much fun we had with others, no matter that we were active in church, we didn't have a good marriage.

I blamed it on all those years of Bill being gone. When he came home, he just began working around the clock, seven days a week. He had a goal, and nothing could deter him. I was just as alone as I had been while he was gone. It seemed to me that he just didn't want to be around me. But nothing can excuse the way I dealt with it, or rather, didn't deal with it at all....

Nobody ever loved their kids more than I loved Cecil, Jimmy, Kenny and Billy. I wasn't mean to them. I just simply did not do my job. I should have concentrated on them, and made them the focus of my life. I was just too immature to realize that.

My home became a trap, and it seemed as if there would never be anything else in life. I grew weary of the routine. Concerned only with my own lack of happiness, I couldn't put my boys' welfare first in my life. I slipped into a depression that my family didn't recognize. When I began therapy, they thought it was unnecessary. It was not. I just could not cope, at the time. I quit square dancing, and teaching Sunday School.

When I first began visiting Mary Catron, it was those fun, early morning coffee times, after we got our kids off to school. If the kids were home, either on Saturday, or when school was out, they went with me.

As I became more dissatisfied at home, I began going to her house, or other places, more often, and staying longer. Too often,

I left the boys on their own. After all, Bill was right there in the back yard. They were perfectly safe....or so I thought.

I trusted my boys beyond common sense. I believed what they told me. I never knew they were out of control at home. I didn't know the older ones ganged up on the younger ones.... especially Billy. No doubt, he was threatened into silence. And I can't blame the kids. They had no stability in their lives. They didn't realize it, but they took it out on each other.

There's no particular time that I can say I came to my senses. All I know is that it went on far too long.

After the boys were all grown, I began hearing the "funny" stories about what was done while I was gone. I was horrified that I had been so negligent. I was ashamed to have been so ignorant. I was the guilty party.

Recently, Cecil Joe Jr. started to tell me about something he had heard. I asked him to please keep it to himself. It hurts me too much to face the fact that I was not a good mother.

I played with them. I took them places. I gave them things. But I failed to give them the daily attention that kids need from the time they are born, until they leave home.

When my sons shower me with love, as they always do, I feel it is an undeserved gift, generously given....one that I cherish...one that I could have lost.

Grandkids, I want you to read this over and over. If my book accomplishes anything at all, I pray that this chapter will get your attention on this matter. Your children are the most precious things in your life. You will not have them with you for very many years. Don't mess up!

Chapter 10

THE JOYS OF RAISING BOYS

D ramatically speaking, I could say that I woke up one morning, and found that I was the mother of three teen-aged boys. But that would be too dramatic. What actually happened was that I woke up one morning, and found that I was the mother of three teen-aged boys! Thank God, Billy was younger.

It was an experience, to say the least. I was unprepared for the job, but it was mine, anyway! Little League became big league! It was that time in life that my mother had waited for, when she could sit back and laugh, and tell me "Now, you are paying for your raising!"

Cecil, Jimmy and Kenny were still working for Bobby Johnson when Cecil began dating a little girl by the name of Debbie. Her mama was single, and had a boyfriend. The boyfriend just happened to be with the Labor Board. Debbie talked too much about Cecil's job. The guy used her to get information, and then filed charges against Bobby. The result was that he had to go back and pay the boys the difference between what they had received and what minimum wage should have been. Over the period of 2 or 3 years it had been, it came to a large sum of money.

Bill and I were angry over the situation. We have always felt that teenagers should be able to work at a job of some kind, for whatever they can earn. If a company had to pay minimum wage, they would hire a man, instead of a kid. We talked to the boys about it, and told them our view on the subject. They agreed with us that Bobby would give them the checks to clear himself with the Labor Board. Then, we would give the money back to him. And that's what we did.

The house was still full of boys around the pool table. But all of them found girls more interesting than pool. Jimmy found out

Vickie was more than just one of the Illingworth kids that came over with their folks. Kenny just liked girls, in general! He looked like Elvis, and had no problem getting attention from the female population....All of them! Cecil has always been a free spirit, and he gave us fits. It was the 60's, the time of the Hippies. And he was a teen-aged hippie....Just as he is now a Senior Hippie!!!! Rebellion was his middle name.

Then, there were cars and motorcycles and school sports to keep me on my toes.....or in the emergency room....and creative antics that required me to reserve a chair in the principal's office, as I visited Mr. Dawson on a regular basis!

Cecil's junior year, 1967-68, he decided to play hookey the day of mid-term finals. Since there was no chance of him passing those subjects without the test grades, we made a drastic and unwise decision: We sent him to Louisiana to work with Speedy. We had no idea that he would have no supervision whatsoever. Barbara had moved in, part time, with Speedy, and his attention was diverted to other matters. His parenting skills were worse than ours!

We took a vacation that summer, after school was out. We were on our way to Tennessee and picked Cecil up on the route. Then he came home to his second year as a junior with the class Debbie was in.

January 29, 1969 was my Mama and Daddy's 60th anniversary. We gave them another party. While we were making preparations at the Ramada Inn for the reception, Cecil and Debbie were out in our car. He failed to make a turn, and wrecked it. Because we didn't have time to shop around, Bill just bought one....that green monster that gave us nothing but trouble.

I could write a book on raising teen-aged boys....But this book is supposed to be about ME!

Jimmy was good at track, but he excelled in football. He made the A team his sophomore year, something that just isn't done... Of course, he was smaller than the other boys. But he had spunk as a kid, that gave him an edge over better little-league baseball players. That same determination made him try harder, and hold his own on the football field. So began my days as the mother of a football star…That was my only claim to fame!

The main role of a Football Mom is to sit in the stands and cheer for her son. But behind the cheering was always that fear that this might be the night that her boy got hurt in the rough sport. I tried to imagine how it would feel to see my son lying on the field, not moving. It was a scene that I prayed I'd never have to witness. And every time a boy got hurt, I held my breath until I saw that it was not my Jimmy.

One night, it was my Jimmy. The stands grew silent. I felt arms of friends wrapping around me. I didn't run onto the field as I had seen other mothers do. I wanted to, but I was paralyzed where I stood.

All these years later, I remember my fear, my emotions. But I don't have any memory of the actual injuries that Jimmy experienced. I do remember the ambulance picking him up on the field. The rest is a blank. Just too many other things, later on, took precedence in my mind.

In the spring of 1969, I was sitting in my folks' living room, visiting with them when a siren pierced the air. To this day, I remember thinking that it was for one of my boys. I had no sooner put it out of my mind than the phone rang, and I was told that Jimmy had been in an accident, and had been picked up by an ambulance.

I jumped into the car and sped to the hospital. A patrolman put his siren on, and pulled up beside me. I rolled down the window and yelled that I was going to the hospital. He backed off, and waved me on. I thought that was nice, but it would have been nicer if he had led me. I found Jimmy in the Emergency Room, waiting to be taken to surgery.

The facts emerged that he had been on his motorcycle, riding with his friend, Cooper Boylan. They were going west on the old highway in Iowa Park, when a car backed out of a driveway into their path. Jimmy dodged the car by taking the opposite traffic lane. Cooper took the ditch side. But the man backed all the way across the highway, into the lane Jimmy had taken to avoid him. The impact threw him over his handle bars, into the car, and onto the pavement.

Jimmy had multiple injuries, both internal and external. The most obvious were the broken bones in both arms, and the crushed wrist. Dr. Pace put the bones back together to the best of his ability, with the understanding that more surgery would have to be done later.

Eventually, he was allowed to come home, with casts from his wrists to his shoulders, on both arms. He went back to school some of the time. When he couldn't, the kids would bring his work home for him to keep up his grades. To pass the hours when he couldn't do anything else, he sat at the piano and played, using only his fingers that extended below the casts. Dr. Pace told him it was good for his healing.

Periodically, he returned to the hospital for more surgery, the most serious being the process of cutting bone from his hip, and grafting it to his wrist. Dr. Pace put him back together with the skills of an artist.

Jimmy was determined to play football the following fall.... And he did! When he made a touchdown, the crowd knew what it meant to him, and the whole town cheered. He even made the All-State team. But I wasn't about to be one of those bragging mama's....of course not!

Obviously, God still thought I needed more experience. A short time after Jimmy's accident, it happened to my Kenny, only there was no other vehicle involved. He just lost control of his motorcycle, and went into a ditch. When he fell, his face hit a broken bottle. He had no broken bones, but his beautiful face was scarred for life.

Yes, I 'allowed' my sons to participate in dangerous sports, and ride motorcycles. Who knows if I was right or wrong?

Cecil and Debbie had been wanting to get married ever since he came home from Louisiana. Finally, Debbie's mom, Ruth, agreed, even though she was just sixteen. Their plans were that they would finish school together, like Bill and I had done. Ruth and I worked together and gave them a beautiful wedding in early August.

Later that same month, we got word that our dear friend, Bill's first boss [on the pipeline] that we came to love so much, Peewee Vaughan, had died. We left immediately and drove to Humboldt.

Peewee had often said he could not be a Christian, because he was not good enough. But he believed in Christ, and he did everything that a Christian should do. He thought because he drank, he could not go to heaven. I recall one conversation when he was telling me "I know I'm not a Christian, but I pray, and I know God hears my prayers."

I said, "Peewee, you are a Christian, whether you know it or not!" His face lit up, and he smiled. I believed what I was saying, and I still do. The Bible says there will be no drunks in Heaven. Of course not. God perfects His own when he takes us home.

Dennis and I stood looking at his daddy's body in the casket. There was a smile on his face. I told Dennis he was smiling because he made it!

...home town boy they all loved...

Chapter 11

THE CITY AND BILL GILMORE

For a lot of years, Bill had worked out of his shop in the back yard. He had so much business that he had to hire help. With the load of keeping up with oil field welding, and repairing trucks and trailers, he regularly worked as long as he was allowed to, legally.

In fact, he was the reason a new ordinance was enacted. It stated that all noise from a business must cease at 11 pm. The neighbors were tired of listening to trucks and welding machines at all hours, and seeing light flashing from a welding rod. Needless to say, they complained. It was bad enough that the block across the alley had become a parking lot for trucks, but the disturbance was too much.

Anybody who knows Bill Gilmore knows that he doesn't like to be told that he can't do something….So, he began looking for a place to move his business. He found a small acreage beside the new highway that he had helped build. And step by step, one building at a time, a few acres at a time, it became Gilmore Inc. rather than Bill Gilmore Welding Company. At first, I was allowed to share in the dream. I designed the office, and it was my domain. I ran it. It was beautiful, until I left….

I can't recall who all the original employees were, other than Jack Capps, Leon Denton, and Jesse Allen. Many came and went. Others stayed. In the 1970's, at one time, there were over 50 employees. Of course, that included our sons, as they graduated from school, as well as Jim Wiese, and Larry Tepher. Then, there was that young man, John Bennett, who came by one day, asked for a job, and never left!

There was a time when Mona Leath, the girl that had become Mike's wife, took my place as secretary. Eventually, another girl by the name of Kathy Smith joined the office staff, and outlasted all of them!

I'm jumping ahead in my story. But the birth of the company, as we know it, was the first event in a new stage in our lives.

During this same time, Bill and Bobby Johnson decided to both run for the city council, as a joke. But the old people in Iowa Park didn't think it was a joke. They remembered Bill as the home town boy they all loved...the one who would help anybody in need.... the one that would stand up for them, when they needed a voice.

Bobby didn't get elected. Bill Gilmore won by the largest margin ever recorded in the history of the city. Oh yes, I was proud of him. But our lives were never the same. From that day on, Bill was a public figure.

Over the next decade, he was involved in the political world that covered not just Iowa Park, but the county, and the district. There were conferences and workshops across the state that required his presence. And through that association, he became friends with many well-known leaders. He was well-liked and respected for his input and opinions.

Being married to Councilman Gilmore was a merry-go-round. If he wasn't at work, he was at a City Council meeting, or a Muleskinner meeting, or a Fire Department meeting.....if not actually fighting a fire. I had to make an appointment to see him!

Chapter 12

LOSING MY MOTHER

No matter what else happens in life, there is no other experience so traumatic as losing one's mother. I had always heard that, but had no idea of what it meant until it happened to me.

Life was going along normally and fairly quietly. Cecil had joined the Marines in December of 1970, and had been sent to San Diego for basic training. Debbie was pregnant with Cecil Joe, and we were all excited. Mama had begun to plan for this great-grandchild from the day she heard the news.

Mama and I had grown apart over the years. There were random times of closeness, when we really had fun together. But as a rule, we did not have a real mother-daughter relationship. Certainly, I loved her, and I knew she loved me. But when my life was falling apart, she didn't understand. No doubt, I failed to understand her needs, as well. I had no concept of her daily life, always taking care of Daddy. I just took her for granted, the way kids always take their parents for granted.

One day in January, 1971, Mama got up, dressed, and went to downtown Iowa Park. She dropped in to visit many of her friends in the various stores. She was laughing and feeling good.

Late that evening, somebody called me and told me that Mama was very sick. I rushed over and found her in extreme pain. I rode with her in the ambulance to the hospital. From there I called my siblings. Keith had Nina there from Oklahoma City in just a little over an hour. Charlotte arrived sometime later. We all just sat and waited, not really understanding that we were losing our Mama.

I have struggled with this chapter for two days. Even after over 35 years, I can't talk about the emotions that overtook me when Mama died.

The rest of my family arrived. We did all the necessary things. I don't remember any of that. I just remember finding my sons and Keith, all hiding in different places, crying. And I remember trying so hard to get Cecil home for the funeral. But in basic training, he would only be allowed to come home if it was a parent or a sibling....'immediate kin'. So his grandma was not immediate kin? He had to go through it alone.

Among those friends who came from a distance were Dennis and Jo. At some point, I said to Dennis, "I don't think it would hurt so bad, if I had just been closer to her."

Dennis looked surprised, and answered, "When Daddy died, I thought it wouldn't hurt so bad, if I had not been so close to him."

What it amounts to is that no matter what kind of relationship a person has with a parent, when that parent is gone, there is an emptiness that is never again filled. I became an orphan when Mama died.

In the years to follow, I learned so much more about Mama than I ever dreamed of. She was a magnificent woman. If I had only known that I was being raised in the presence of greatness....

Somewhere among all the stuff I've written over the years, there's a book containing "The Candy Dish". It was written as a story. This account is simply meant to be factual. It's complicated, so follow along with me....

Following the death of Mama, we agreed that my siblings and I would take turns staying with Daddy. Lillie stayed first. We had cleaned the house, and divided many of Mama's treasures among us, so that whoever was there would have less dusting to do. It was a mistake, because Daddy missed all those little things being there. We just didn't realize it.

All my life, Mama had a beautiful iridescent depression glass candy dish, always displayed in a prominent place. Anyway, while I was visiting with Lillie one evening, I told her that I had not seen the candy dish that had been in mother's curio cabinet in the living room.

Lillie said, "Oh! I know where it is! Mama gave it to Bertha. And when I tell you why, you will be glad!" Then she told me the story.

Bertha Ward had been Lillie's friend ever since the two families lived at Skellytown where I was born. She lived in Dallas after she and Ward married. They came to visit Mama and Daddy in Iowa Park on a regular basis.

During one of those visits, Bertha saw the candy dish. She told Mama, "That dish is exactly like the one my mother had when I was a child. I don't know what ever happened to it. I didn't get any of her things after she died."

After Bertha left, Mama worried about what she had said. She began trying to remember when and where she got the candy dish. And finally, the memory came to her....

When Mama was pregnant with me, Bertha's mother was also pregnant. As women did then, they agreed that when their times came, they would help each other deliver. I came first, and Bertha's mother was there. Then, it was Mama's turn to help her, when she had twins.

There was also a doctor present. He delivered a baby boy, and laid it aside, telling Mama, "This one is dead." Then, he delivered the second boy, and said, "This one will live." He gave the baby to Mama to clean up, as he was leaving.

As soon as he was gone, Mama put the healthy baby down and went to the kitchen. She put water on the stove to heat before she got two tubs out, working as fast as she could. She filled one tub with cold water. Then she filled the other one with the hot water. She hurried back to the dead baby, picked him up, and began a primitive shock treatment, of placing him first in one tub, and then the other.

Eventually, the baby cried! My Mama had saved his life, after he had been declared dead!

The baby's mother was so grateful, she wanted to do something to show her gratitude. Mama would not have taken money, even if any had been available. But finally, she accepted a gift of love… the candy dish. It was the woman's most prized material possession.

Over the years, Mama forgot where the dish came from. But it also became her most prized material possession.

The next time Bertha visited her, not long before she died, Mama placed the dish in her hands, and told her, "Your mama gave it to me, and I want you to have it."

I know the story turned out just the way it was meant to be. But Lillie was wrong about one thing: I still want that candy dish!!!

Chapter 13

GRANDMA MARYANNE

It seems that each time death took someone out of my life, new life was added to it. The years to follow were filled with life and death, and constant change.

Three months after Mama died, my first grandchild, Cecil Joe Jr. was born April 28, 1971. I was 39 years old. It was the beginning of a whole new role for me. Nothing can bring on 'maturity' like becoming a Grandma!

The next month, Jimmy graduated, and started making plans to go to a technical school in Nashville. I had not adjusted from Cecil being gone to the service, and now Jimmy would be leaving, too.

When Lillie went home, I stayed with Daddy, leaving my family at home. Sometimes, Billy would spend the night, but I missed being at home with all my boys and Bill. When school started, Billy couldn't stay with me at all, because Daddy would wake him all hours of the night, just as he did me.

School had only been in session about a week when I was called to go home for a very important conversation. Sixteen-year-old Kenny had a problem: his girlfriend, Becky Willis, was pregnant. I found the old expression, 'I felt like the floor fell out from under me,' was totally accurate.

Becky's mother, Ramona, came to the house to talk about options. Maybe to others, the answer might have been abortion, or giving up the baby for adoption. But both were out of the question, to me, and to Bill. A few days later, before the Justice of Peace, they were married.

Suddenly, I had gone from having a houseful of boys to just one little boy. Billy then had to learn to take care of me, all by himself! And he did a good job. He's still taking care of me!!!

Before we knew it, the calendar had to be replaced, and 1972 arrived. April 12, just one year after my first grandchild arrived, we had our beautiful Angel.....Angela Dawn.

Vickie graduated from High School in May. She and Jimmy got married in June. It wasn't long after their wedding that Bob and Bonnie moved to Waskom. Our life patterns were changing rapidly.

It was sometime during this era that my brother Glen was diagnosed with a little known disease called Alzheimer's. According to what we were told at the time, Alzheimer's was a deterioration of the brain, similar to senility, but affected people in their 50's and 60's, much earlier than the senility we were familiar with in old people. It was also said to be confined to those with brilliant minds, who spent their lives thinking constantly, never allowing the brain to rest. That fit my brother exactly. Over the next several years, we would see him change into a stranger.

In later years, Alzheimer's became a household word for regular Senior senility....a far cry from the unknown disease that enslaved Glen.

Life still goes on, and I encouraged Marvel to have a social life, rather than to become trapped in Glen's strange world.

I can't remember exactly when my "modeling career" began, but it was in the early 1970's. Bill and Kenny and Jimmy all became Charter Members of the Rotary Club in Iowa Park, which automatically put the girls and me in the women's auxiliary, the Rotary Ann's. For some reason, Becky and Vickie thought they were too young for society life, so I usually had to attend those meetings alone.

At one luncheon, we were to bring guests, and a dress shop from down-town Wichita Falls held a style show. I took Pat Leath as my guest. I had been asked in advance if I would model for them. I was scared to death, but I did it! Each model wore a sports outfit, a tailored suit and an evening dress. It was fun, and the clothes were beautiful.

At the end of the afternoon, the dress shop owner asked me how long I had been modeling…. I told her, "Oh, about an hour!" We both laughed, and she said, "Really? You do it so well, I was wondering if you would like to work for me in the future."

Well! Yeah…..why not? I had quit my job at the shop. And Billy was almost grown. So I did a few shows for her at other organization's meetings. I got paid by choosing one of the outfits to keep as my own. But when she needed me seemed to be the times when I couldn't do it. So, as much as I enjoyed the limelight, my 'career' ended. And I was just plain 'Grandma" again.

....Mother's Day, 1974...

Chapter 14

GOODBYE DADDY

The time came for me to stay with Daddy again. Believe it or not, it was harder than it had been before. He resented me going to work, and wanted me to stay at the house with him all day. During the previous months, I had undergone a hysterectomy which brought on early menopause. So it was pretty rough, regardless of my love for him.

Daddy's attention-getting antics were sometimes amusing. But there came a time when it was not funny at all. I was at work when one of the neighbors called me. Daddy had gone to the front door in his wheel-chair, and began shouting, "HELP! HELP!" Of course, he was heard, and several people ran to the house.

When I got there, and saw that there was nothing wrong, I was very angry with him. That led to me telling him that he was making it impossible for me to stay with him. In turn, he said he didn't want me with him, that he would rather be in the rest home. He had no idea that I would follow through on that, but I was at the end of my rope. I called Bill. He came, and before the end of that day, my daddy was in the rest home. I collapsed in utter defeat.

Of course, when I went to see him, we both apologized. It was then that Daddy made a suggestion that seems to be the perfect solution:

He said he didn't really want to be in the rest home, and why couldn't he move into our house with Bill and me, and Billy? He wanted to rent his house to Kenny and Becky, who were living in the old Brittain house next door to him, and the rent would go toward them buying it after he was gone. I asked him if he was sure that was what he wanted. Yes, he said, that would be the best for all of us.

I told him to stay at the rest home a while, so that we could make the necessary changes in our den entrance from the carport, and into the adjacent bathroom for his wheel chair. We did that, and bought a new table and chairs to go in the den, so that we could all eat there with him. We set up his bed in the other end, so that he could navigate that one big room, without having to go up the two steps to the rest of the house. All of it was done as quickly as possible, so I could bring him home.

When I wrote to my siblings about the arrangements, some of them rushed home. Daddy told them that I had stolen his house from him, and they believed it. The matter was taken out of my hands, and Daddy was put into the rest home again....for the rest of his life. So, his final trick proved to be the factor that took away his freedom. There was nothing I could do about it.

As he deteriorated, it became harder and harder to visit him. I would no sooner recover from the emotions of seeing him like that than it was time to go again.

Mother's Day, 1974, Bill and Billy took me out for lunch after church. Then, we went to the rest home to see Daddy. We found his lifeless body lying on his bed. I kissed him and told him it was okay. He was out of his misery. I felt such a relief for him. I told my Daddy Goodbye.

Less than three weeks after Daddy died, a new grandbaby arrived. Cecil and Debbie had a little girl May 30, 1974.

If I had ever had a little girl, I was going to name her Hope Elaine.....not after anybody, but just because I thought it was a beautiful name. At some point, in Debbie's pregnancy, I had mentioned that to her mother, Ruth. It seems that Ruth told Debbie. Both agreed they liked the name, too. Without me knowing, they choose it for this little girl. So, twenty something years later, I got my Hope Elaine!

December 21, that same year, 1974, Kenny and Becky had our precious Kenny Glen Gilmore Jr. I really loved the role of Grandma. There was a lull in the baby factory for a while.

Chapter 15

LITTLE GRANDMA

Over the years, Bill's Mama, lovingly known as Little Grandma, had been a huge part of our lives. Sometimes she would come spend a few days with us, and disappear as quickly as she came.

One of those visits extended into many weeks, to our delight. She would be up before the crack of dawn, fix her own breakfast, and go back to her room before we ever stirred. We always found little notes she left for us, such as the one that read, "Have dined on sumptuous leg-o-lamb, and retired to my abode...."

We had installed a swimming pool in the back yard just about the time our first grandchildren were born. She loved sitting by the pool, even though she didn't go in it. Once in a while, she would dangle her feet over the side. But what she liked best was sitting out there after dark, with the moonlight on the water.

If Bill happened to be gone to one of his meetings, I would sit with her for hours. I remember her tiny body perched on the end of the diving board, with her knees pulled up to her chin. Sometimes, she was lost in thought. Other times, she talked endlessly about her young days. She would tell a story, and laughter would shake her whole body so much that I was afraid she was going to fall off the diving board.

May 20, 1975 was her 80th birthday. We had a party for her at our house. And what a party it was! All her friends from nearby were there. Kenny and Becky had gone after her brother, Uncle Gus and his wife, Aunt Lota, and that thrilled Little Grandma.

Uncle Deck and Aunt Pearl lived in Odessa, where he was in a rest home. Aunt Myrtle had heart problems, and a pacemaker had been installed, so she was not able to travel, even from Irving, where she was staying with Rena Mae.

Uncle Gus and I were visiting in our den when he said to me, "I sure wish we could see Deck just one more time."

I replied, "Well, if you want to go, Billy Joe and I will take you. We can go by and see Aunt Myrtle, too, and take you home from there."

He got excited, and asked, "Do you really mean that?" I told him to just ask Billy Joe. Of course, Bill said yes.

Uncle Gus told Aunt Lota, and she got excited, too. Then he ran to the living room where Little Grandma was. "Mae!" He shouted at her, "Billy Joe and Maryanne said they will take us to see Deck and Myrtle! Do you want to go?"

Little Grandma yelled, "YES!"

We asked when they wanted to go, and the answer from all of them was "Tomorrow!" So, we got up early the next morning, and took off on a journey we have never forgotten, with three octogenarians!

They were as lively as teen-agers, and laughter filled that blue Cadillac from front to back. They never got tired, and ate such things as Mexican food and pizza, and lots of ice cream. Uncle Gus sat beside me in the front seat, with the two women in the back.

The reunion in Odessa was touching to watch. We all knew it was the last time the three siblings would all be together. Aunt Myrtle was the only remaining member of their family. We all wished she could have been there too. But at least, Little Grandma and Uncle Gus would get to see her.

The long, wide, straight stretch of I-20 between Odessa and Fort Worth is an open invitation to let the gas pedal hit the floorboard, and BJ doesn't even need an invitation! So, on the way to see Aunt Myrtle, his foot got really heavy. Inevitably, we saw the black-and-white coming toward us, and cross the median just behind us. Bill just pulled over to the shoulder and stopped.

All three of them asked, "What are we stopping for?"

Billy Joe just laughed as he was opening the door, "Oh, I just need to see this man about a dog...."

The women were first to turn around and look behind us, and see the flashing lights of the patrol car. Both of them began to protest, "Why is he stopping us? Billy Joe wasn't speeding!"

Uncle Gus chimed in as well. He needed to go back and tell that man that Billy Joe was not doing anything wrong! It took quite some convincing from me before they were willing to face the fact that their innocent little boy was indeed guilty of the offense!

That Cadillac was the best car we have ever owned. Beautiful, heavy enough to hold the road, and it felt like riding in a rocking chair. No bumps were ever felt, even in the back seat. So our passengers had no idea that they were traveling at 90 miles per hour. Of course, if they had been aware of the distance between cities, and the short travel time, they would have figured it out! It was worth the price of the ticket to hear them all defending Bill.

We continued our trip on to Irving, and observed another great scene, with sisters and their brother together for the last time those three would be together, too.

Little Grandma decided to stay with Aunt Myrtle at Rena Mae's house for a while. So the next day, we drove Uncle Gus and Aunt Lota on to their home in Wills Point. We returned home happy, knowing that we had given Bill's mama the best gift we could ever hope to give her.

The year 1976 was our country's 200th Birthday, and the celebration was to go on all year. Billy would be graduating in May, along with his girlfriend, Denise Wooten.

One day in February, Little Grandma called me, and said, "Ann, I'm sick. Come get me." I was there in the time required to drive across town. I took her by the clinic to see Dr. Soell, who told me to get her to the hospital immediately. By the time I had her checked in, he was there. I called Billy Joe and Veneta. They came, and stayed with us until bedtime. Then both left, because they had to work the next day.

I knew without a doubt that she was leaving us. But her children were in the same denial mode I had been in when MY mama died.

I couldn't tell them what was happening. All through that night, I sat with her, and from time to time, she would call out, "Ann...." She was the only person who was allowed to call me Ann. I would go to her and take her hand. She would squeeze as much as she could, and we just held on to each other.

Early the next morning, I called Bill, and told him to come right then, saying he needed to be there when Dr. Soell got there. He didn't understand how important it was, and ran an errand first. Veneta came to see her mama 'on her way to work'. Dr. Soell had arrived a short time before, and I had left the room. I caught Veneta, and tried to tell her one more time. She just stared at me with unbelieving eyes.

As we stood there, Dr. Soell came out of the room with that look on his face. He walked up to us, put his arms around both of us, and cried "We have lost her!" I don't know how long we stood there.

I knew that doctor loved my mother-in-law. I had seen it many times when I took her for her check-ups. She would tell him something funny, and make him laugh. I had seen him look at her with adoring eyes, just as if she had been his mother. So when he said, "We have lost her", and stood crying with us, I knew he had lost a dear friend, rather than just a patient.

I wish I could say I handled her death with wisdom and maturity. That would be a lie. I fell apart, and made some monumental blunders. We all fell apart.

Saying Goodbye to Erma Mae Beauchamp Gilmore was not an easy thing to do.

Chapter 16

A NEW CHAPTER

No matter how sad life is when we lose those we love, there are always happy times ahead.

March 11, 1977, Kenny and Becky gave me another grandson, Kelly Joe Calvin. There was still room on my lap.

I don't remember the date, but we were invited to a wedding at Dallas in 1978. James Illingworth was marrying a beautiful, tall, wonderful cigar-smoking liberated girl by the name of Laurie. She won our hearts instantly, and became as much a part of our family as James had always been.

In the fall of that year, Debbie announced that she was pregnant again. Christopher Clark came into our world, April 21, 1979.

Another event, April 10, 1979, just 11 days before Christopher was born, made a lasting mark on all of us. That was the day of Terrible Tuesday, the huge tornado that wiped out a great portion of Wichita Falls, leaving many of our loved ones homeless. Veneta and Bill were among those who had to move into government trailers while their homes were being rebuilt.

Soon after the tornado, Billy and his friend, Randy Hughes took advantage of the risen waters, and were boating down the Wichita River toward Wichita Falls. They came across a muddy mess of a dog trying to dig out of the bank. They rescued it and brought it home.

Our beloved dog and cat, Gomer and Lightening, had both died a short time before. So, there was room in our home and hearts for another pet.

When we got her cleaned up, we discovered the most beautiful Sheltie we had ever seen....or ever would see. She had tags, and after a few phone calls, it became obvious that her owners didn't really want her. They told me her name was Fanfare. But to me, she became just plain Fannie.

Even though Billy rescued her, she was MY dog! It was at least 2 months before she would let Bill touch her. Wherever I was, she was with me. When I sat down, she was at my feet. We were inseparable.

I'm not sure about the reason behind the conversation, but I think Bill was pushing Jimmy and Vickie to have a baby. Jimmy told him, "When we have a boy, I'm going to give him a hammer and screwdriver, and let him play on your new dining room table…"

One day, the two of them came in with big smiles on their faces. Jimmy laid a hammer and screwdriver on the dining room table…. His way of announcing that Vickie was going to have a baby!

We hardly knew that Vickie was pregnant before we got the call that she had her baby, at least three months early. Jason Bradley was born May 27, 1979. He was small enough to hold in one hand, and lived in an incubator for the first few weeks. Vickie went home from the hospital without her baby, but she and Jimmy were there in the nursery as often as they were permitted. So were the grandmas and grandpas. We did a lot of praying for that tiny little boy. There were a lot of sighs of relief when he was allowed to go home with his mama and daddy.

Chapter 17

COUNTRY COLLECTIONS ART GALLERY

1979 was also the year that COUNTRY COLLECTIONS came into being. I had told Bill that I needed a life of my own, rather than just being Mrs. Bill Gilmore. He asked what I wanted to do. I said, I wanted to open an art gallery. He agreed, and helped me get a bank loan for the building that was put on company property.

My idea was unique at the time, though it was soon copied in many places. The building was a beautiful barn style, with a porch across the front, and a swing on it. It was very inviting. I used our old furniture, and created the interior look of an old house. There was the living room by the front door. The dining room and kitchen were beside it. Across the room was the bedroom and sewing room.

Across the back, I installed an old fence-post divider, making a separate place for Jack Steven's sculptures. He was the only well-known artist I had in the beginning. But I had sent letters to all the art associations, inviting local artists to display their work on a commission basis.

I spent a lot of time preparing for the Grand Opening, hanging pictures and arranging the different areas. It looked great. The day before opening, I was flooded with late coming artists, who discovered that it was going to be a real gallery…..and the Grand Opening itself would get lots of attention. I accepted those late additions, and worked all night, getting ready for the next day.

The opening was indeed grand! The city had a delegation there, and a council-woman cut the ribbon…..I made a speech…..yeah, I did! And I was in business.

There were so many stories created at Country Collections that it would require a book to relate them all. It was an exciting and fun time for me. There were newspaper articles written about my adventure, and I met a lot of the elite citizens.

Since I owned the gallery, it was assumed that I was an expert in the field of art. So, I had to do a lot of studying, and I did learn about all the media and styles….even abstract painting! And there were some abstracts hung in my 'living room' that were really good. I should have bought one of them, myself.

The hardest part of it all for me was refusing bad work. In the 'sewing room', I had hand-made items, much of it crochet. And, everybody thought they could crochet! Some of the stuff I looked at would have made good cleaning rags!

One of the TV stations had a show that high-lighted local businesses, and Country Collections was chosen as one of those. The hostess was a girl by the name of Lori Ann Crook…..before she moved to Nashville and teamed up with Charlie Chase, as Crook and Chase

After she became famous, I tried to get a copy of the program. The station told me that it was not possible. Later, I heard that Lori Ann had filed an injunction to keep them from distributing her work there, because it was too 'amateur'. Well, I thought it was pretty professional, myself!

I guess the most expensive piece of art I had was a finger-painting by a little girl named Hope. It hung above my desk. It was priceless….Still is, and it's mine!

Country Collections was a regular hang-out for many artists, and the coffee pot was always on. Business was good in the beginning. But as much as I hate to admit it, I failed to be strict enough in the contracts, and as time passed, many of them used the gallery as free display area. Since I had their business cards on their work, the public began to call them directly, to see if they would sell a piece from my gallery at a lower price, cutting me out of my commission. It didn't take long for me to catch on. When one artist in particular began to take his work off the walls just after a customer showed interest in it, I confronted him. He admitted it, and I told him to take it all, and don't come back.

As a business woman, I should never have put their cards on their work. Galleries now keep that information from the public. I just trusted people too much. I learned things I didn't want to know!

But at the same time, I gained confidence in myself and the experience taught me more than I could have learned in four years of college. I met people that I would otherwise never have known, both as artists and customers. And among my favorite customers was a young plumber by the name of Mitch Miller.

Oh yes! Having the gallery also brought invitations to gallery shows across the country, where artists displayed their work. Most of those I ignored. But when one came for a show at the Superdome in New Orleans, I couldn't pass it up. Pat went with me. We had a ball. I saw parts of New Orleans that I didn't get to see when I lived there! And, we drove by the house I had once lived in. It was still there.

...a dream... kept in my brain...

Chapter 18

CHAPEL CHURCH

During the same years as when I operated my gallery, there was another role I needed to fulfill.

At church, there were many children in the worship service without their parents, due to the bus picking them up. Mike drove the bus, and therefore he sat with those children during the services. But they were disruptive and he had a hard time controlling them. So, for a while, Bill and I tried to help him. That led me to the decision to act on a dream I had kept in my brain for a long time.

I have always felt like the children's church in most places is just a glorified baby-sitting service, to keep kids out of the sanctuary. It was my desire to create a service for children that duplicated those in the adult worship services.

I took my ideas to Glenn Schell, who was also the Educational Minister as well as our choir director. He listened to me, then sat back in his chair and said, "Lady, you are the answer to my prayer!" He added that he had wanted that kind of program for a long time. He gave me full responsibility for securing a staff of people to work with me, and free reign to organize the program. And, we would use the Chapel in the basement. So, that's how I came up with the name of Chapel Church.

Most of my staff was easy to choose. First of all, there was Bill, and of course, Mike. Then I asked Preston, and he was delighted to be a part of it. We found a piano player, and Mike would lead the singing. Preston represented the Deacons. We needed a preacher. I made a mistake in that choice that proved to be a constant thorn.

The man was a friend that I thought could relate to children, and who himself felt he had been led to preach. It was a disaster, because he had no affinity with the kids at all, talked above their heads, and refused to follow the outlined program that would teach the children the meaning of everything that took place in the Sunday Morning Worship Service in the sanctuary. Instead of studying the outlined topic, he insisted he had to "preach what God gave him" each week. It didn't take me long to realize he was listening to the same radio preacher I heard each Sunday morning before church, and repeating that message to the children, even though they didn't have a clue as to what he was saying.

I admonished him several times, telling him that he could not use language like "the Inspiration of the Holy Spirit" to little children. It did no good. All I can say is that the rest of us were able to reach those kids in spite of him.

Just like in 'Big Church', we had a song service, and the offering before the message, and an Invitation at the end. The little boys took turns 'passing the plate'. The children were proud of putting their pennies and nickels in the offering plate as it came by them.

Preston, with the help of friend Bud Thompson, built a beautiful little altar. Many children gave their hearts to Jesus at that altar.

I had requested that the age begin with those in school, so that all of them were beginning to read, and could follow the Bible reading, with help. At our highest point, we had around 90 children on our roll. When they became 12, they were supposed to go upstairs. But many of them pleaded to stay, because they loved Chapel Church….And they loved us.

Chapter 19

THE GOOD LIFE

As the decade of the 1980's began, it seemed as if we were on top of the world! Business was good, and we had enough money to do the things that were important to us. We were blessed with friends and our family. We were both involved in the community and church life.

In February, 1980, Bill and I celebrated our 30th anniversary with a trip to Hawaii, staying on the island of Kauai for a whole week. It was fabulous. And that's all I can remember! At least, I have pictures.

Billy and Denise declared their independence July 3.....the day before the Nation's celebration. It was a 'hurry-up' wedding...It sure was! Billy wanted Denise to go along on a motorcycle trip with Jimmy and Vickie. Society had begun to accept co-habitation by then, but we were glad that they wouldn't make the trip together until they were married. So, after four years of planning, the wedding was rushed up!

There was a time of sadness during the Labor Day weekend of 1980, when Glen died. We mourned not for the empty life that had replaced the vital man, but for the brother I had adored. But, like Daddy's death, it was a relief to see Glen released from his suffering.

During those years, I cooked Sunday dinner after church every week, and most of the time, all our kids were there. We had lots of little grandkids running around. Sometimes, we had other guests, too. We thoroughly enjoyed it.

Life was good.

...citizen of the year...

Chapter 20

OUR WORLD DESTROYED

In the fall of 1981, Bill came to me and told me that he was being investigated for wrong-doing. He said he was guilty of making false tickets for an oil company, so that the local superintendent would get the difference between the actual charges and the amount of the invoice. He did it to keep the company business, of which the man had control. That was the total benefit to Bill. I forgave him, and told him I would stand by him.

My business at the gallery had become a pleasant place for people to spend an afternoon and visit. But sales were slowing down, mostly due to the dishonesty of many artists, as I explained in an earlier chapter. I closed the gallery, and went back to work for Gilmore Inc. We moved the offices into my building. At the time, there were three other secretaries. The company employed roughly 50 people in the various shops.

January 11, 1982, Cecil and Debbie had their last child, another baby girl they named Heather Leigh.

A few days later, I was contacted by the Chamber of Commerce, and asked for my assistance in surprising Bill at the annual banquet to be held late that month. I was speechless, and unable to tell them it was a bad idea.

Nina was visiting me at the time, and I confided in her about my dilemma. She told me to accept the request to help honor Bill, because he had earned it, and even if the worst happened, he should be recognized for all the good he had done.

At the banquet, Frances George was chosen to present the award for CITIZEN OF THE YEAR to Bill Gilmore, in recognition of, not only his contributions to the various organizations and churches, but also his help to individual people over the years.

Within weeks, all hell broke loose. Bill was indicted for, of all things, mail fraud, in a federal court. No matter that he had no part in any mail fraud...in fact had not mailed any invoices to the oil company, but rather gave them directly to the supervisor...because the company mailed payments to Gilmore Inc....they were able to twist the charges.

We could not leave the house without being harassed by reporters or cameras....just as in the case of public officials we had observed previously, when they were being prosecuted...and their families persecuted! Since that time, I have had an empathy with politicians who are going through similar situations. I don't question whether or not they are guilty, because I know that in the minds of the public and media, it doesn't matter. It's just a big story.

It is not my purpose to defend Bill for the actual wrong he did. And this book is not about him. But the fact remains that he became a tool in the hands of a group of people with an agenda. When I asked his attorney why they were going after him, rather than the people who were responsible for the theft, his reply rocked me on my heels.

He said, "Does anybody know those men? No. If they were prosecuted, it wouldn't make the news. They want a 'big fish', and what better way to get publicity than to go after a successful businessman who is active in church, a city councilman of 12 years, a Rotarian, a volunteer fireman, a public servant who has just been named Citizen of the Year!"

During the so-called investigation, a girl was sent to our office to apply for a job as a secretary. She got the job, as she seemed qualified. However, her real role was to gather 'evidence' against Bill. At the grand jury hearing, she testified that Bill kept two sets of books, and one set was filed under lock and key.

Anybody who knows Bill Gilmore knows that he keeps nothing under lock and key, and to ask him to organize anything into files is a joke. It's all on top of his desk. And keeping books is not now, nor ever has been his department. But that and other lies were told.

One of our employees was an ex-policeman who had been fired. He was offered....and received....a position in a distant town as a deputy sheriff in exchange for his false testimony.

There is no need to discuss the 'trial'. It was a farce. Everything had been decided with the judge before it started. Bill was sentenced to 18 months in prison. He would be required to serve 9 months before being eligible for parole.

In May, 1982, Billy, Denise and I drove him to the Texarkana Federal Prison, and watched him enter the gate to the main building. After processing, he would be moved to the minimum security facility for 'white-collar crime' offenders.

As my grandchildren read this, I want you to know that your Grandpa was not sent to the prison facility for what he did. He was convicted because of who he was. By today's standards, he should have been fined, and given "community service" to perform. But what more community service could he have done than what he was already doing?

Bill met some fine people who, like him, had been targeted for some political purpose. One was an Oklahoma County Commissioner who was guilty of accepting small gifts from people. Our own friend and County Commissioner Buck Voyles, told us that he could have been prosecuted for the same offense, since he often accepted such things as eggs or garden produce from his friends across the county. It's only when it benefits somebody's agenda that it becomes a crime.

Another life-time friendship Bill made at Texarkana was that of his counselor, Tom Gregory. Tom was a good man, the only one in the facility that seemed to be interested in the individual. He was compassionate and respectful of the inmates as people.

I'm still trying to overcome the bitterness toward those people who knowingly contributed to the destruction of MY world. Therefore, I will not relate the emotions I experienced. It's in the past. Nevertheless, my family was put through hell, and that was worse than what happened to me.

I lost my cherished Chapel Church…guilt by association. When I faced our pastor, he said the church was splitting over me. I told him, no, it wouldn't split over me, because I was leaving. And I did.

Although they kept the name I gave it, Chapel Church today is a far cry from the ministry we had. In fact, it is exactly what I didn't want it to be….a glorified baby-sitting service.

June 7, 1982, while her grandfather was at Texarkana, Kenny and Becky's baby, Karlee Janiece was born.

The business suffered drastically. Bill's defense had cost an enormous amount, and of course, there was 'retribution' to be paid, even though somebody else took the money. So we were in bad shape. But the boys and I, along with Kathy and John held it together. We wrote letters to our creditors, promising them that we were not going to take bankruptcy, even though many people were trying to break us. Most honored our credit. We made it.

Later that year, I became severely ill. Each time I visited Bill, it seemed that I had an attack that I felt I just could not live through. On one such visit, in November, Bill's siblings and spouses went with me. I left them in the visiting room with Bill, and went to the bathroom.

There was a chair in the corner, and I sat there, doubled over with my head near the floor. A black woman came in, took one look at me, and said, "Oh honey! You are sick!"

I said, "Yes ma'am, I am." She walked up to me, laid hands on me and began praying. The pain began to subside. I couldn't stand up, but I motioned for her to bend down, and I hugged and kissed her. She stayed with me until I was able to go back to the room where the rest of them were. They never knew what had happened.

On the way home, it hit again. I was curled up in the back seat, trying to keep from screaming. None of them, Bill, Veneta, Buddy or Jerry realized how badly I was hurting, and decided to stop beside the road for a picnic. I thought I would be dead when they got back to the car. But I made it all the way home.

Immediately, I called Kenny….I don't remember why he was the one I called, but he was there quickly, and rushed me to the hospital. Within hours, my gall bladder had been removed, and I was on the road to recovery.

My good health was short-lived.

In January, 1983, I finally convinced Dr. Soell that there was something seriously wrong with my passing blood through my bladder. He made an appointment for me with Dr. Charles Dryden. After one examination, Dr. Dryden told me my left kidney had a mass in it, and would have to be removed. I was sent straight to the hospital for surgery.

The report came back that it was malignant. Somehow, I already knew it. They had gotten the majority of it by removing the kidney. And they were able to get what they found in the arteries. But bits of it were in the capillaries and couldn't be removed.

Somebody contacted Tom Gregory, at the prison. He worked to get permission for Bill to come home. He was to go to work at the shop during the day, and spend the nights at the new Half-way house at the Salvation Army. His parole date was in February.

When Bill got to the hospital, he called the Salvation Army and told them where he was, and that he would check in before evening. "No," the Power in Charge stated, "You will report in NOW!" He had to leave me at the hospital. It did no good for Tom to make the arrangements for him to be with me. Bill was told in no uncertain terms, "You are OUR PRISONER, NOW!"

When I went home from the hospital, I was alone. Bill was not allowed to stay with me. He came to the house before work, at noon, and again before going back to the "Half-way House". That was against the Salvation Army's orders. They threatened to send him back to the prison if he was caught at the house.

For some reason, I no longer support the Salvation Army. For an organization that preaches Christianity and compassion to treat us in that fashion was unforgivable

Though the contact has slowed in the past few years, we still receive Christmas cards from Tom Gregory, and the two men talk on the phone from time to time. He and his wife are planning to visit us at our Oklahoma retreat in the near future....hopefully before my book is finished.

At the time of my illness, Renal Cancer could not be treated by Radiation or Chemo. The only effective treatment was said to be Interferon, which would not cure it, but would retard the spread. Although Dr. Dryden tried to reassure me, by telling me that one patient had lived 20 years, I had a hard time getting past the report I found from the Texas University Medical Center that stated that Renal Cancer was always fatal, and the life expectancy was two years.

While I was in the hospital, Kenny and Becky separated. Each of them came to see me, but not together. When they happened to be there at the same time, I saw their faces, and knew, without being told. So, I had that to contend with, all the while I was making plans to die. Later that year, they did divorce. It broke my heart.

As you know, I didn't die!

Bill later received a Presidential Pardon. But nothing could ever make up for the damage done to our lives.

All we could do was try to salvage as much as possible, and learn to live with the changes that came about in our family, business and social life. If we had allowed it to destroy our faith in God, we could never have survived the tests that were yet to come.

END OF BOOK III

Book IV

Table of Contents
Book IV
Comedy, Tragedy, and Serenity

Chapter:

...hilltops and valleys...

Chapter 1

PICKING UP THE PIECES

Well...we had hit bottom and there was no place to go but up. The fact that Bill and I both knew I might not make it brought us closer together. He began to take care of me, literally. It was time to get on with our lives, time to try to forget what had happened, and begin living again.

Our social life was certainly different, since we no longer belonged to the Rotary Club, and Bill retired from the Fire Department. He stayed in the Muleskinners, and devoted a lot more time to their functions, but still was home much more than in previous years.

We had always had a lot of friends, but now we were able to separate the TRUE friends from those casual, fair-weather variety. And, little did we know that we were yet to develop many relationships of great value, some with people still unknown, but others we had known for years, without really being close.

Our future most certainly would still contain hill tops and valleys. We just had to learn not to live in the valleys, but to climb back to a higher place where we could see around us, and thank God for our blessings.

I went back to work at the shop, lying on the couch much of the day. Still, it was better than being at home, and there were things I was able to do. Business got better again. Then, we had to watch out for all the people who thought we were a fair target for cheating, by not paying their bills. Lawsuits became a part of our routine. Most, we won. But it was a hassle and expensive to retain lawyers.

The best thing to happen that year of 1983 was the birth of our last grandchild for many years. Vickie and Jimmy had their little girl, Bobbie Lynn, September 17, 1983.

Bill is a much more forgiving person than I am. He wanted to return to our church. I just couldn't do it. So, we bounced around for a while, trying this one and that one.... Presbyterian...Church of God.....Assembly of God.... We were accepted by most of the people, but in each of them, there were still those who looked at us with contempt.

We became involved with a small group trying to get the old Chapel from Sheppard AFB moved to the Expressway. But that didn't last long, due to conflicts.

Eventually, we did return to First Baptist in Iowa Park. We still had many friends there. Mainly, Pat and Preston, and their kids wanted us back.

I learned to smile when one or another of those hypocritical souls gushed over how happy she or he was that we were back. I think the Lord forgave me for silently addressing them as 'bitches... or sons thereof....' If not, I'm confessing my sin right now!

Chapter 2

WHO'S WHO?

The chapters in this section of my book overlap by necessity, as many things were happening at the same time. Before continuing with tales of my life, I must insert some vital family information. Otherwise, the subject matter will be interrupted with explanations.

At home, our life took an unexpected turn. Kenny married Linda, and a long battle began with Becky, over the kids. In the conflict, Bill and I gained custody of Karlee.

Linda was older than Kenny, and had three children. The girls, Audrie and Jolynn were both older than Angel. Victor was the same age as Kenny Glen.

Kenny got the other three children. Kenny Glen and Kelly also lived with us a great deal of the time. Angel was with us for short periods.

Our home life consisted of many grandchildren, but Karlee lived with us for almost 14 years. Heather and Bobbie Lynn were her best friends.

Audrie had Timothy, John and Jessica before my blood grandchildren began having families, and before my own last grandchild was born. Her last little boy, Adam, was born much later.

April Fool's Day, 1994, granddaughter Hope had a little boy, Bobby Clark Best. Hope and Robert would later divorce, and Bobby stayed with his daddy in Michigan.

July 1, 1994, our very last grandchild was born when Billy and Denise had Lilah Rose.

Cecil Joe Jr. and Jana had Cullen McKensie May 6, 1995, and Cadence Mae arrived January 6, 1997.

Angel was married for a few years, but is single at this time.

Hope married Matt Best some time after her divorce. Matthew was born January 28, 2000, and Patrick came March 9, 2003.

Victor was married for a while, and has one little boy, Dillon.

Before Kelly married Sandy, she had Jenny and Jessica. Dusty was born May 11, 1998 And Jimmy came December 28. 2000. Kelly and Sandy are now divorced.

As of this writing, none of the other grandchildren have children.

Jason and Julie got married in 1999. Soon after, Christopher and Allison were married, but I can't find the date. Heather and Mark were married in October of 2001.

Karlee was married to Jacob Robertson September 28, 2002, at our Oklahoma retreat.

Neither Kenny Jr. nor Bobbie Lynn have ever been married.

Chapter 3

PROWLING IN THE PROWLER

Vowing to make the most of the rest of our lives, Bill and I talked about what we would really like to do. Travel was at the top of the list. That kind of involved the purchase of an RV, since I wanted very much to go camping, and Bill didn't like tent camping.

I don't remember where we found that first beautiful little Prowler travel trailer. It was absolutely the most convenient, most comfortable arrangement we ever found in an RV. The living room consisted of a sofa-bed on the back wall, facing a huge, floor to ceiling picture window on the opposite wall. We could sit inside, and be outside all at the same time.

In the summer of 1984, my family had a Chambers Family Reunion in the Wichita Mountains. One of my favorite memories from that time was all my siblings crowded into my trailer…. The couch packed on that wall, and chairs lined along the window wall, all of us facing each other with feet touching. There was a lot of stories and laughter.

Lillie quieted us all down, and said, "I have something to say, and then we are not going to talk about it anymore…. In November, I will be 75 years old."

All of us siblings sat stunned, and just looked at our sister. It was sobering to realize that she was getting so old. Our mama was 79 when she died. So, we reasoned in our heads that we would have our oldest sister another 4 or 5 years.

Our very first vacation in the Prowler was to Red River, New Mexico, a short time after my family reunion. We traveled as we pleased, when we pleased, and stopped wherever we pleased. We had never before had a vacation like that. It was wonderful.

We returned home that September day in 1984 to a tragedy. Mona had died. Mona Leath was Mike's wife, our precious young friend….one of our secretaries….and Bill's staunchest supporter in time of trouble. The whole Leath family was our family. We felt the loss personally.

For many years before Bill and I bought our first Prowler, Pat and Preston had been traveling in their RV with Bud and Billie Thompson. Now, it was time for us to butt in….and we did.

I forgot a story that needed to have been told in those chapters when Bill was working overseas, and my boys were growing up.

Bud and Billie lived…..still do…..just across the block to the north of us. There came a time when I couldn't handle a situation with my kids. Why I called Bud the first time, I don't remember. But from that time on, when there was a problem that needed muscles to solve, I called Bud. He put the fear of God into my boys…. and it was always a while before I needed him again.

After my boys were grown, Jimmy joked that he was 14 years old before he learned that Bud was not his DADDY!

So, the Thompsons were good friends, before they also became family to us.

I should be able to recall all the great escapes we made across the country in a caravan with our friends. There were just so many good times, it's hard to pin down one special vacation. Maybe it was to Branson….. or maybe it was to Big Bend…. or maybe just to the Wichita Mountains in our own area. Wherever we went, it was the best time we ever had!!!! My sister, Charlotte, even joined us once, in her motorhome.

We also branched out on our own from time to time. There was one January, maybe 1985, that Nina and I stayed in the Wichita's alone for two weeks…. There was snow on the ground, and nobody around, except for the rangers who came to check on us once in a while. We would bundle up and take walks around the park, with my little Fannie. We put out a birdfeeder, and watched the variety of birds come to our windows. It was an experience I have never forgotten.

That first Prowler got messed up in a storm. But there were other travel trailers in our future….and other travels…..

As my grandchildren grew into traveling companions, we took them camping in the Wichitas many times, either all together, or in small groups. A couple of times, I did it all by myself…..

The first time I packed the pickup full of grandkids and took off. I had barely parked, and was getting all the bicycles out of the trailer. Karlee was among the first to have hers. Our parking space was different from our usual spot, and she wasn't expecting the curve to meet her so soon. She crashed, and had to be taken to the hospital. I left the rest of the kids in Angel's care, and rode with her in the ambulance…..it was quite an experience. But we both lived through it!

Another time, Karlee was away for the summer when I took Kenny Glen and Kelly with me. It was one of those times when I was lucky, and parked the 32' trailer on the first try, with Kenny Glen directing me.

Shortly after we had settled down, a couple of young men pulled up with a tiny little camper. They tried to park it next to us, back and forth, back and forth many times. Finally, the boys told me they were going to tell those guys that Grandma would park their trailer for them!!!

I was able to convince them that it was not a good idea!

There came a time when we went shopping for a new RV, and made the mistake of taking Karlee and Bobbie Lynn with us. Those two little girls could manipulate us, even when we didn't want to be manipulated! But it was all too easy for them to convince us that we needed that Hotel on Wheels…. a huge trailer with a big roll-out, before such became regular RV design….

When parked, the living room, dining room and kitchen were as large as some of the homes we had lived in during our young years. The bathroom and master bedroom were both spacious, by RV standards. But the selling point was that bedroom for the grandkids....with bunk beds, and their own dinette that made another bed....and yes, their own TV!

I have to admit it was a beauty, and a joy to stay in. However, there was one small problem: We couldn't park it in regular spaces. When we tried to travel in it, we were parked wherever it would fit. In one case, that meant in the road!

A few years after we let it go, we had a perfect place for it! But that's another story.....

Chapter 4

HIGHLAND CEMETERY

Two things happened in 1985 that would each change our lives. I don't remember which developed first, but it doesn't matter. I will start with the subject that is the most difficult to relate.

Bill came in one day and told me that he had been asked to take the position of president of the Highland Cemetery Association. My first reaction was "No! I don't ever again want to be in the public eye!"

But he then said, "Honey, I have always wanted this town to be proud of me. Maybe this would be my chance to regain the respect of the people, and to do something that would make up for my mistakes."

I said, "Okay. If that's the way you feel about it, then go at it!"

Needless to say, he went at it in typical Bill Gilmore fashion: He made the decision that he would see to it that the cemetery became a place of beauty, rather than the run-down, weedy expanse, where many stones were overturned, and others were covered by trees or bushes. He began not just overseeing the meetings, as was expected of him, but exerting his own physical labor, on a volunteer basis.

I caught his fever, and began trying to work with the caretaker to clean up the little shack where all the tools and 'records' were kept. Just one look at the recipe box of 'records' told me what a mess it was in. My parent's lot listed Mama as the owner, but didn't show Daddy's burial. The Gilmore lot had my little baby, Kelly Len, listed as the owner of the lot! Obviously, there was a lot of work to be done.

The man resented both Bill and me for our interference, and quit. That left me in the position of learning the whole cemetery operation immediately, and taking over the sale of lots, keeping records, and over-seeing burials.

I worked around the clock, trying to create books where there were none. First, I went to the woman who had been the association treasurer for over 40 years. I asked to borrow her ledger, so that I could trace the owners of all the lots. Although she worked in a bank, she didn't keep a book listing the sales of lots, and who paid for them. So, I asked for the bank statements and cancelled checks.... which were always returned with the statements at that time. Her face turned red. She gave me bits and pieces of boxes.....nothing in order.....nothing complete....and no cancelled checks. She said she had thrown it all away, because it wasn't needed. Needless to say, she also resigned.

The story has been told that there was a fire at the cemetery in the 1940's that destroyed all the records up to that time. And nobody had bothered to keep accurate records since.....

I went to the funeral home, and traced every burial I could find, all the way back to Jesse Tanner's records from the early 1900's. But not all burials went through his funeral home. And many of those records were missing, too.

My next chore was to start calling people who had relatives buried in Highland Cemetery. I would say, "I need your help in confirming the burials on your lot, and the ownership." Some were helpful. Most were annoyed. Many were indignant that I didn't already have that information. And more than a few were downright ugly to me. Without alarming the public, I couldn't just say, "There are NO RECORDS!"

Bill and I were both living at the cemetery after office hours, late into the night, until we could no longer work. I was trying to tend to the cemetery business out of our company offices. I sat on the floor, drawing maps of the cemetery, and entering known graves in the correct places.....all on company time. I walked the entire cemetery, space by space, entering the information on charts that I had made at Gilmore Inc. expense.

Eventually, I told the association that I could no longer justify that much work on a voluntary basis, and I would have to quit Gilmore Inc. and be employed by the cemetery, full time....or give up my work there. I took a pay cut of some $50 per week.....and officially became the cemetery supervisor....or whatever title fit.... at less salary than the caretaker that didn't take care was paid!

We hired another caretaker.... Matthew Wallace, the little boy who had grown up at my house, Corliss's son. We were a good team.

I had a dream of a beautiful pavilion, with an office and tool room included. I presented my idea to the association, and was given the go-ahead, if I thought I could accomplish it! I drew my plans, and took them to a member of the association who was an architect. He transferred my plans to a blueprint. Then, I began a campaign to raise the necessary funds.

The effort was contagious, and many people volunteered their talents, time, and labor to the project. Of course, my husband was at the top of the list, and coordinated all the work. Our dream came true.

I wish I could end this chapter on a happy note. But as always happens when somebody works hard to create something of beauty and pride, there is someone else just waiting to start telling them how they should be doing things. Dissension began to erupt. A few trouble makers can ruin the work of endless hours and dedication. And my joy of all I had done in the cemetery was destroyed. I quit in 1988.

Today, few people remember what either Bill or I did. Nobody is aware that I brought about the birth of the Pavilion, or that he uncovered the east end of the cemetery, repairing stones as he went along.

The association is still in an uproar, more than 20 years later.

...motorcycle riding cat...

Chapter 5

A HOG IN OUR GARAGE!

Jimmy had always wanted to own a Harley Davidson dealership. He had applied some ten years before, and was told that he was too young. So another man got the franchise. But over the years, he didn't satisfy the company expectations, and in 1985, the dealership was once again up for grabs.

After some negotiations, Jimmy, Mike, and their friend, Jim Weise, applied for the honor, and got it. My art gallery building was the new home of Red River Harley Davidson.

Mike and Jim Weise both decided they wanted out of the deal, as in those first few years, it was not a promising venture. Mike didn't want to quit his secure job at the telephone company, and Jim Weise decided he would rather be a policeman. So, Jimmy and Vickie became the sole owners.

Well, anyway…. Bill and I were looking at the company catalog of motorcycles when we saw a picture of a red Harley with a sidecar. No matter that we had never ridden motorcycles….except for a small one Bill had for a short time as a kid. After all, this one was RED, and it had a SIDECAR for our little dog, Fannie….and maybe even our new kitten that had joined our family in January. That's all it took….We ordered it!

By the time our new toy was delivered, almost a year later, my little Fannie had died. So, on our virgin excursion, we put Tinkerbelle in her carrier, and carried her in the side car. We were breaking in the motorcycle, and ourselves, at a slow speed on a 1500 mile trip through Louisiana, Mississippi, Tennessee, Arkansas, Oklahoma, and back home to Texas. We all three loved it.

There was a world waiting for us that we had never even dreamed of! When we made our first Poker Run, we met the most wonderful people who immediately made us feel like part of their group. These people knew how to have fun.

Our image of the motorcycling community had not been very flattering. We assumed that we were getting into an awkward position of being church-going citizens mixing with a bunch of brawling drunks! Did we ever have an education coming, and our new friends taught us well! These people went to church, too, and very few drank at all, and none of them were sots!

That first year, we decided to enter the ABC's of Touring contest, in which riders were to gather the names of towns with names beginning with each letter of the alphabet. Each state, and each Harley Rally counted, also. We made the trip, completed the alphabet, and Bill got his picture in the Hog Tales magazine.... with Tinkerbelle, the first known motorcycle riding cat!

A short time later, we adopted a beautiful little show-dog beagle, named Regal Beagle the Second!!! Thus, Bea also became familiar with the side car. And there would be yet another ABC's contest, in which Bea and Tinkerbelle rode in the side car together, across the nation, to Canada, to all the New England states, Washington, DC, and back home. They made good riding companions, and were extremely helpful in the traffic....as other motorists would see a dog and a cat on a motorcycle, and back off laughing, as they let us go ahead of them. We were even allowed to park in a 'No Parking' zone in Washington, by a policeman who wanted to get a picture.

When we got Karlee, we realized that God knew we would need that side-car. Indeed, she grew up in it.

We were charter members of the HOG Chapter. Bill would later be the director, and I became Editor of the newsletter. As Chapter officers, we helped in the planning of the very first Texas State HOG Rally.

Over the years, we experienced adventure after adventure, riding across the United States in every direction, with friends or alone. We became acquainted with the Big Wigs from Milwaukee, mainly through Jimmy and Vickie. We got to go to Puerto Rica with them, where we rubbed elbows with Willie G. and Nancy Davidson, Rich and Ann Terlink, and other officials.... really classy stuff!

But the most valuable part of the entire experience was the life-long friendships that were created during the 1980's through our Harley. We rode for more than a decade with most of them.

I can't name all of them without leaving out somebody really important. Of course, Bob and Bonnie also joined the rides. Preston, too, as well as Mike. Once in a while, Pat would ride with us, but she really didn't enjoy it. Preston's bike was not comfortable. Neither was Bob's, but Bonnie has an iron butt!!! After Mike and Frances married in December of 1988, she also rode with us.

Through it all, our most frequent riding companions were Nick and June Gilliam, and Helen and Richard Robinson. One trip in particular will always stand out in my mind, as the time when we all became extremely close.

We had ridden to Knoxville, Tennessee to a National Rally. It was fun, but the episodes along the way will never be forgotten… such as us getting into a motel that obviously was designed for rental by the hour….not exactly our cup of tea…and we had Karlee with us, too.

Karlee had her 9th birthday during the trip, and we had a party for her in a motel room. The rest of the trip, her beautiful new doll rode with her.

Then, we went to see Roberta, in Nashville. She made my friends welcome, and we spent the night. When I lost my sister, they grieved with me. That's the way it is with true friends.

That HOG is still in our garage, and it's getting impatient to be fed and exercised!!!

...incredible journey...

Chapter 6

THE YEAR OF 1994

That was a year of diverse events. It began with a fabulous Chambers Family Reunion at the new RAC building in Iowa Park that our Billy had birthed.

He was president of that association when the recreation center was an old, run-down barracks in a bad part of town. He led a small group in planning a beautiful, functional building, in a good location. Then, just as I explained in my chapter on the cemetery, as soon as the new building was erected, and the association membership became a status position, there was no problem getting people to join, and tell him what he should be doing with his project. So, he soon resigned.

Nonetheless, we had that reunion in the facility on the weekend closest to Mama and Daddy's anniversary, January 29th. And it was the most successful we ever had, with almost the whole family there.

We had not realized how bad her health was, so it was a total shock when my sister, Roberta, died in March. I had spent a lot of time with her over the more recent years, and we had grown very close.

July 1, 1994, after 14 years of marriage, Billy and Denise finally had a baby. This one would definitely be our very last grandchild... Her name was Lilah Rose. She stole some of our attention from Karlee!

We had been planning a long trip with Speedy and Barbara for at least a year. Finally, it happened. A short time after Lilah was born, they came to our house from their home in Mississippi. And we took off for a three-week journey that would retrace our travels in younger years on the pipeline. Karlee was with her mother for the summer.

Barbara had brought up the subject, telling us that she wanted to see all the places that we talked about when we were together. And the rest of us thought it would be fun to see the changes the years had brought about.

There is a complete journal, and album of that trip somewhere among our stuff. We called it Our Incredible Journey…and it was indeed.

Barbara and I had tolerated each other for years, because we had to. Eventually, we began to like each other. But during that vacation together, we grew to really and truly love each other.

Our route through Wyoming was close enough to Lillie and Woody for us to make that part of our visit. We stayed there a couple of days, and all of us had a wonderful time.

Although we had never lived in the western part of Montana, we decided to make an excursion to Glacier National Park, and visit with Roberta's girls. First, we stopped at Arlee, and set up our tents in Deni's yard. She was married to Taag then. He and the two little boys were great. We were treated like royalty.

Then we drove on to Kalispell, and found Teri and Brian, and their two little girls. Again, we got the royal treatment.

When we started out to the park, we wanted to take the little girls with us. Dakota didn't feel like going. But four-year-old Niki jumped at the invitation. Teri told her she needed to eat before we left. She insisted, "But I'm not hungry!"

Two blocks from the house, Niki announced, "I'm hungry now!" And that set the pattern for the rest of the trip. She entertained us with stories and questions and excitement. If we had not had her with us, we may very well have forgotten the trip by now. But to this day, we all recall that day with Niki.

When we decided to go through Montana, we had to omit some of the places in which we had lived, like Pocatello, Twin Falls, and Baker, Oregon. Instead, we went across the panhandle of Idaho, directly to Spokane. It had changed so much that we didn't know where we were.

From there, we went to Seattle, then turned south to Bonneville, and down the Oregon coast to California. Although it sounds rapid on paper, the trip was slow and fabulous. Everyplace we went was more beautiful than the previous…or so it seemed. Every day was better than the day before.

We drove down the coast of California to Fortuna, and then to the tiny town of Rio Dell…..which wasn't even there! The story was that it had been destroyed twice….once by storm, and once by fire….and had been rebuilt a little farther inland.

By mutual consent, we avoided San Francisco, and drove down the middle of California, through the wine country, all the way to Bakersfield. Then, we turned eastward, and began to put more miles into a day, as time was fast approaching for Karlee to return home.

We didn't go everywhere we had planned, and we went some places that were not in our plans…but there was nothing about the trip that we would have changed.

...all together again...

Chapter 7

CLASS OF 1950

The members of W.F. George High School Class of 1950 had our 45th anniversary reunion in 1995. It was a happy time, as always, when we all got together. We had met every 5 years since we got out of school.

Now it was time to plan for our 50th Anniversary reunion in 2000. So, we decided to get together soon, for a planning meeting. When that meeting came around, we didn't get any planning done, for all the fun we had....So, we had another meeting. Same thing....

After a number of tries, we decided we enjoyed those times so much, that we would just get together every three months, from then on! And that's how our suppers began.

Eventually, we did make some plans....that is, we chose all the people who would be responsible for the different needs. James Hair was our chairman over all of it, and it was then that I began writing the regular newsletters. We worked together to find every last member of our class, regardless of whether or not they graduated with us.

In case I haven't said it before, James and Billy Joe were closest friends in school, and remained so all through the years. Wanda was in the class below us, and we double-dated a lot.

James became a well-known member of the Corps of Engineers, winning recognition for a new technique in constructing dams. In May of 1999, he was inducted into the *Gallery of Distinguished Civilian Employees* by the United States Government. So, it was kind of a strange friendship between the White Collar and Blue Collar....But they were like brothers.

I loved both him and Wanda, and we visited them often, sharing our families growing up years. So, it was easy for me to work with James.

Other classmates that we had been close to all through the years were Walter Spruiell, and Wilma, from the class below…and LaVerne [Giggles] Walters and her husband, Billy Joe Harrington. Patsy Steed and Oscar Singleton divorced, and we lost regular contact with her for some time. But we still talked from time to time, when she came to town to see her parents.

Katy Merle married Morris Vogel, and moved to the Denver area. But distance never dulled the friendship between us. When we were together, we just picked up where we left off. And that's the way it was with the other Laverne….Laverne Talley, who married Jack Backhaus. She has never been able to attend our class events, but we have seen her a few times in Casper, Wyoming, on our way to see Lillie.

Franklin Farmer and I have always been best male-female friends, the kind that can tell each other anything in confidence. We understand each other, and that's worth a fortune. When we were seniors, he told me, "I'm sure glad you don't care about your grades, because I want to be Valedictorian." And, he was.

While he was working with the Sunday School Board in Nashville, he came to Roberta's house a couple of times when I was visiting her, and otherwise, I saw him with his family at their home. The relationship has always been good, but grows deeper as we both age.

Bill and I had become very close to one classmate after we moved back home…Peggy Curlee had married Bull Ansel, and in those years, we visited pretty often. She guided me through some of my early studies in writing, and our whole family loved her a lot. After Bull died, she turned all her attention to selling Real Estate, and dropped her contact with all her old friends. We tried many times, but just could not get her interested in our group. She came a couple of times, and then just didn't want to be bothered any more. It still makes me sad.

One of my best friends in school had become distant to me over the years, and I didn't understand why. During one of those suppers, the men had gravitated to one area, and the women were all at the opposite end of the table. The conversation turned to the issue of problems we had experienced in raising our families. As one or another of them would tell of something painful in her life, others would nod and say something like, "Yes. I went through that, too!"

My friend sat silently, taking it all in. Later, when we were alone, she said to me, "My husband and I have avoided people all these years, because we thought all of you were talking about our family problems."

I was shocked. I said, "Hon, nobody ever talked about you. We were all too busy taking care of our own problems to even know what was going on in our friends' lives."

She replied, "I know that, now." And our friendship was restored to much more than it ever had been as teen-agers.

We became attached to many other classmates with whom we had not visited over the years, except for our 5-year reunions. Some had to be maintained through correspondence, due to the distance. Others were local. There is no way I can name them all, without forgetting some.

In the beginning of our quarterly meetings, we had a regular place where we reserved their private room. Then, one time we arrived, and the place had closed it's doors without notifying us. We waited until everybody was there, and just drove to another restaurant, and seated ourselves at the available tables. After that, we learned that somebody had to check a few days ahead, to be sure the place was expecting us!

Because so many of our members lived in the Dallas - Ft. Worth area, we sometimes met near there. Our group was growing larger with each passing supper. As others were convinced that we were serious about our plans for a BIG BASH in 2000, they grew more interested.

We finally found the one member we had been looking for ever since we got out of school. His name was Johnny Worrell. Each time somebody thought they had found him, it proved to be the wrong man. But research of a Johnny Worrell in Longview Texas found our guy. He was thrilled, and promised he would be at our next supper, which was scheduled in Fort Worth. We were all excited.

We had a huge crowd in that Mexican restaurant, and the table was so long that we couldn't talk to those at the other end…but no Johnny Worrell. We were just a bit angry with him.

The next week, I received a letter from his wife…She told us that Johnny had been looking forward to seeing all of us again, and it had given him a lot of happiness. But he had died during that week before our supper. It broke our hearts. And I guess maybe we learned a lesson. At our age, we should give people the benefit of the doubt, when they disappoint us….We never know when it's beyond their control, even if it isn't a matter of life or death.

We had already lost several of our classmates, including my dear friend, Mary Coleman Catron. And we knew we were at the time of life when others would be leaving us.

The suppers, and my newsletters, led to some very unexpected friendships where the relationship had been casual classmates previously. One was with Paula Ralston, and her husband, Wayne McNatt. Paula was part of the trio I sang with in school. We had always liked each other, but our paths ran in different directions. But now, she and Wayne became regular house-guests, who feel at home with us.

In school, there was one guy, Bill Weiler, the son of a teacher, who was extremely intelligent. We had a couple of classes together, but had not often been in the same group socially.

Weiler was now retired from his position with Core Labratories, and living in Idaho. He had spent many years in Libya and Bahrain, before moving to Singapore as Vice President of the Eastern Hemisphere in the company that became Litton Industries. He was on his 3rd wife when we started communicating.

Her name was Martha. She was, at that time, editor of the Trailer Life RV Guide. A couple of royal snobs, they were sure to be! Oh yeah! When Weiler finally drug Martha over to our house in Iowa Park while they were visiting in Electra, we each decided we could tolerate each other….

As I was checking my facts for these paragraphs, Martha informed me, "Yes, I'm Weiler's third wife. In fact, I knew the other two, and I'm definitely the best!" [I believe her!] Weiler, himself adds that it's okay to have three wives, as long as you trade UP!

Bill had seen Weiler once, while he was in Bahrain. But who would have dreamed the two of them would ever have anything in common? Still, in this past decade, we have become very close friends. They continue to travel around the world, at least once a year, and sometimes two. Yet, they also enjoy the simple life we live.

When the big weekend arrived, other classmates arrived from all across the country. A big swath was cut from all the various social levels, but nothing was important except that we were all together again. And the fun began!

For our Class Dinner, we had secured the most prestigious establishment, the University Club, located on the top floor of a bank building, overlooking the city lights at night. We really dressed up for it! Even the men wore something besides cut-offs and t-shirts!

The next morning, we had a school bus and driver to give a tour of Iowa Park and the surrounding area, with our home-town boy, Jackie Hodges, acting as tour guide. We passed the homes where many had lived, and those now living elsewhere were shown all the new development, including of course…our new prison.

That evening, we all attended the Alumni Banquet at the 'new' high school cafeteria. Paula had decorated our tables, and put place cards on them, so that we could all sit together. And, for the evening's entertainment, we attempted to sing "Old Friends", without crying.

The next morning, we met for breakfast, and bid each other farewell. It was to be the last time many of us would see each other.

James was very tired all week-end. We knew he was not well. But we weren't ready to hear the report of terminal cancer.

He and Wanda spent their 49th wedding anniversary on November 21st at home, without fanfare. He apologized to Wanda for not being able to stick around for their 50th, which they both had looked forward to.

Bill and I went down to that Ft. Worth hospital, and stayed as long as we could. Each of us had a private visit with him, and all the things were said that need to be said. Then, we left Wanda and their boys to endure it alone.

We would have returned, but James said he just didn't want any more goodbyes. He died November 28th, 2000, just two months after our celebration.

December 6, 2000, recognition of the service and death of James L. Hair was read into Volumn 146 of the Congressional Record by Representative Martin Frost.

Chapter 8

OLD FRIENDS

L ittle did we realize that our 50th reunion was just the beginning of more serious relationships for the rest of our lives. Our quarterly suppers attracted more people, and soon we began to include members of the classes above and below us.

Pete Koonce was the first permanent addition to our group, from the class of 1949. He was already a very dear friend to many of us, so it was just natural for him to come to our suppers. And several of the spouses were from other classes, and their classmates were invited, too. Many from the class of 1951 joined us, on a regular basis.

Bill and I had been close to Jackie Hodges' little sister, Joyce Perkins, and her husband, Bob, for a long time. They were probably the next to be adopted into the circle of Old Friends. Jackie's wife, Barbara Tatum was several years below us, but some of her classmates joined us, too. One of those was the little sister of our own Jimmy Arnold...Frances, and her husband Pat Taylor.

Jimmy had never changed from the fun-loving character he was when we were young. He and Nona had divorced in the years since we experienced the tornado incident. It was good to hear that they remain friends. And it was good to have him back around us again.

Pug and Gerald once again became as close to us as when we were in school. Virginia Partney and Jackie Banks had been together all the way through high school, so I refrained from chasing him..... He was literally the most handsome young man I had ever seen.... well, except my brother!

Seriously, although I really liked Virginia in school, I was never around Jackie enough to know him well. That changed with our regular suppers. He was now a handsome, bald headed man, with a heart of pure gold. I'm sure it had always been there, but I just had not been aware of his loving nature. And he was the next classmate to leave us.

I thank God for those few years of true friendship. Virginia continues to make the effort to be there, as hard as it is for her, alone.

Peggy Fox had been a neighbor of Bill's, and had dated Buddy before she met her husband, Johnny Moore. They had missed the 50th celebration, but later began coming to the suppers. It was a problem for them, because they had a booth at the Flea Market in Bowie on the same weekends we met. But once they learned what they were missing, they decided to close early on Saturday, and join us.

Leonard Whisenhunt…yes, the boy I was engaged to…and Nettie had also missed the 50th Reunion, due to her health. They were finally able to go to Decatur for our supper. They asked Bill and me to meet them at their motel, and accompany them, since he felt he would not remember anyone, and Nettie only knew a few Iowa Park kids in school. So, we did. However, Leonard found that he was not a stranger among our classmates. That began a very valuable friendship.

A short time later, in September 2003, Angel was living in Oklahoma City, where the Whisenhunts also lived. She had back surgery, and wanted me to be with her. Nettie insisted that I stay with them. I explained that I should get a motel, because Karlee and Kenny would also be with me. But they both insisted that there was room for all of us, and they would be hurt if we didn't stay with them. So, we did.

It was a very stressful time for Karlee, Kenny and me, at the hospital. But both Nettie and Leonard made us comfortable, and helped in every way possible. Later, Angel had another trip to the hospital, when none of us had time to get there. Leonard took care of her, as if she was his granddaughter. We will always be grateful to both of them.

The last classmate to join us for our Lunch at Tranquility Place…. [we got too old to be out after dark, and had to change the time…] was Joyce Nell Beck Truitt. She was able to attend our 50th, but living in Florida didn't allow for casual trips to supper. But recently, she and John moved to Ardmore, Oklahoma. We plan to see each other more often in the years ahead.

There are so many others that I can't begin to name them all, who became regulars at our get-togethers. Precious friends.

Ruby and Dean Simmons were visiting us one time at Tranquility Place when she mentioned that she and Peggy Fox had been best of friends as kids. I immediately contacted Peggy by e-mail, and was able to put the two of them back in contact. They continued to communicate until Peggy died, in June 2006, as I was writing this book.

Her death was a shock to all of us. Pug and Gerald, and Betty Perry McGinnis joined all the Gilmore siblings, and me, at her funeral in Hennessey, Oklahoma.

That's the way it is with Old Friends. We don't know who will go next. But we cherish this time we have together, and continue to thank God for the bond between us.

...old tree lying on its side, still living...

Chapter 9

A QUIET RETREAT

Life had grown tedious again during the year prior to the new millennium, with heartaches and trials. In the year of 2000, our 50th Wedding anniversary weekend at Quartz Mountains was a terrible disappointment for me, although our kids had fun.

My grandkids all had chosen to go out on their own, and my nest was empty again. I was about to crash under the worry and stress. I told Bill I had to find a place of our own, to get away from it all. I wanted a place to park the travel trailer, for long periods of time.

Billy located a place for sale in Missouri on the Internet. We took off, and drove up to look at it. The fifty acres were on the side of a mountain, and although it was beautiful, it wasn't practical for our purposes. So, we drove home through Arkansas, jotting down the information we found on "for sale" signs along the way. It was Saturday, and all the offices were closed. When we got to the Oklahoma line, we quit looking.

We were just about to Durant, and I was studying the map, just out of curiosity. I told Bill, "Instead of following US 70 through Ardmore, like we usually do, let's take that little Oklahoma highway 32 that goes to Ryan."

He shrugged his shoulders and said it didn't make him any difference. We weren't in any hurry, anyway. So, at Kingston, instead of turning toward Madill, we went straight west, toward Marietta.

We were just Sunday driving along, on that Sunday morning, enjoying the scenery when we saw a "for sale" sign. Instinctively, Bill turned around in a driveway, and went back. The entrance was hidden by trees, but there was a beautiful iron gate. Of course, it was locked, but we saw an older mobile home, and a small shed. The driveway was long, with trees making a canopy over it. It was pretty, but I told Bill it was too close to home. He said, "Well, I'll call tomorrow anyway."

We weren't sure if the sign said 10 acres or 70 acres. The latter would be much too large for us. But Bill made the call, and was told that the place was under contract, but the man would like for us to look at it, as he thought maybe the people would not be able to get the financing. So, the next day, we drove back up to Marshall County, Oklahoma.

The agent had opened the gate, and as we drove up to the mobile home, we passed a grove of trees that just begged for RV spaces between them. We weren't really looking for any buildings on the property we wanted, but we might consider it, anyway.

We discovered a huge barn behind the house. The inside of the mobile home was okay, too, certainly not fancy, but comfortable. We saw lots of potential. We fell in love with the big deck on the front, and the picture window that overlooked it.

Once again, I told Bill that this was closer to home than I had wanted. He said he thought the distance was just right, because it was near enough for me to drive back and forth, yet far enough to be removed from all the problems at home. I finally agreed.

Once out on the deck, I looked to the west, and gasped. There was an old tree, lying on its side, still living, while sprawling across the ground. I said, "Bill, look! There's your mama's tree...."

He looked at it, then back at me, smiling. "Yes, it sure is!"

The agent said, "Oh, it wouldn't cost much to have that thing removed!"

We just laughed, and I said, "If we had this place, nobody would touch that tree!" Then we told him about the tree we had sat in while we were courting....and that our kids had sat in it, too.

That tree is what sold us on the whole property. Bill told the agent, "If the other people don't take it, we will."

We were told we had to wait 30 days for their deal to either be finalized, or cancelled. As we drove out the gate, I asked Bill if he really wanted it. He said, "Well, I'd like to have it, but I'm not going to set my heart on it, because I don't want to be disappointed."

I answered him, "Well....I'll tell you what: If the Lord wants us to have it, we will get it. And if He doesn't He will have another place for us that will be better." Bill agreed. We drove off with the decision to forget about it, and let things happen as they may.

We went to our Chambers Family Reunion in Colorado, and had a wonderful time. As soon as we got home, we received the phone call that we were the lucky people who were going to buy that little acreage. We got into the car again, and headed for Madill to settle the deal before we told our family.

Quietly, we moved enough of our furniture to make it possible to sleep in the house, and sit in the living room. The kids were excited for us, and each came when they could. We swore them to secrecy, until after we had a chance to surprise Bill's siblings.

...a little bit of heaven...

Chapter 10

TRANQUILITY PLACE

For years, Veneta and Bill, Buddy and Jerry, and the two of us had been taking turns every month, hosting outings to various places, trying always to do something unexpected. It was our time to host the others, and when we got to the gate, we told them that friends had loaned us the key, and told us to spend the night….They bought it, until we walked into the living room, and Jerry recognized the couch. She yelled, "YOU BOUGHT THIS PLACE!!!" Of course, the secret was out.

That weekend, we discovered that we were 6 miles from Lake Texoma….As time passed, we learned that Lake Texoma is a nationally recognized recreation area, and lots of famous people live around here. But all we cared about was the fact that we had found a little bit of heaven.

Pat and Preston were among our first friends to come up for a weekend….and instantly became part of our plans and dreams. He and Bill worked together on the things they could handle alone.

One time, they had gone around the acres, putting up Bluebird houses in various places. Then Preston came into the house to rest. Pat went back outside for something, and I had gone into my bedroom. One of the bird houses was just beyond my bedroom window to the east. It had not been 15 minutes since it had been erected. But what I saw made me yell, "PRESTON! COME HERE!"

He ran into the room, and joined me at the window, and we stood talking softly about the Bluebirds that were already inspecting the house. After a few minutes, I realized that the door, which needed a doorstop, had slowly closed. I casually walked over and opened it….Pat was standing there, wondering why her husband was behind that door, whispering to me….Yeah, she bought our story!

We were enjoying sharing our place with our family and friends. But there were some important additions that needed to be completed before it was ready for inviting a crowd. Bill still had his priorities right, and had a washer and dryer installed, even before we were staying for long periods. How thoughtful of him to think of me!!!

As all the areas of serious work began, we soon had a standard crew on hand.... Mitch Miller, Dean and Ruby Simmons, and Clarence and Iris Hill. Mitch, of course, was our friendly plumber. Sometimes, Kay would come with him. Dean had been our family carpenter from the beginning of our home in Iowa Park. Ruby was his live-in helper, and often dropped by to check on his job. She and Bill had grown up as neighbors, and I liked her a lot. But as the weeks of transformation took place, we became as comfortable as old shoes. Most of the time, Kenny was also here to help. Kelly also was on hand when he was needed.

The bathhouse was the first addition, following the installation of those RV spaces. As soon as one thing was finished, another started. Kenny placed his own RV on the property, and began to spend a lot of time with us.

The time came when we wanted to invite our classmates to our place. Our first supper had to be served in our back yard. They loved it as we did. Paula and Wayne had a hobby / business of tole painting items which they sold at craft markets. They agreed to paint cute little signs for the driveway, and that began their visits with us. In fact, they were the ones with the winning name, which they had already painted on a sign which was a gift to us... TRANQUILITY PLACE.

We first invited our Old Timers, as we call those friends who were in the first batch of Harley riders with us, before the whole Chapter came....They wanted another invitation.....and got it.... and another....Bob and Bonnie always came up a few days ahead to help us get ready.

In the midst of all my new-found happiness, there came a week in October, 2001, that knocked the wind out of me...All in one week, I lost three of my dearest friends. The first was my childhood friend, Sandy Williams...I didn't have time to absorb that loss until I learned that Corliss had died....Then, it was Ruth, Debbie's mama. All three were a vital part of my life. And all three were suddenly gone.

During the summer of 2002, Karlee announced that she wanted to have a garden wedding at Tranquility Place. And she wanted that wedding in September! And she wanted it beside the pond that her daddy had just dug a few months before.....

Don't know why that would be any problem. All we had to do was erect a gazebo, find a gardener, put plants on the dam, get lights to shine on the water....Oh, yeah....Go shopping for a dress, cake, invitations.....and make out my list of guests.....

It all got done, with Kenny's help. His gazebo base would rival any commercial deck. When we got through, the place was so beautiful that I wanted to get married there!

There is a short story somewhere, about my nearly fatal accident two weeks before the wedding. I forgot something on the stove, and let a skillet catch fire. Because I had done it at home, I was determined not to burn my kitchen up again.

Stupidly, I picked up the 6 lb, 1" rimmed "skillet" full of blazing grease, and started outside. As I reached the door, I slipped in grease that had spattered on the floor. I landed on my back, with my knees bent, still holding the skillet of fire level over my body.

I told the Lord that I couldn't die just then, as I had a wedding to take care of. He agreed.

I had to reach through the fire to pull myself up by the door knob. I threw the skillet out into the yard before I discovered I was so badly burned that there was nothing left of my robe.

There is no doubt that an angel was there with me. I made it through a rapid recovery, and walked the distance between the house and the wedding site on the 28th of September.

There were countless miracles connected to that event, and I have never forgotten that God was in control.

Other than that September day being above 90 degrees, and our air condition failing in the house….and me walking outside to answer a question without my blouse on…..and forgetting to put my make-up on…that wedding went off without a hitch!!!

Special guests were Becky and her little boy, Marcus. Ramona, and Paul were there, too. It was the beginning of a time of healing for all of us.

Another year went by rapidly. Then, in August 2003, we suffered another heartbreak, when our precious friend….my friend from our early Skelly roots, the son of my parents' best friends before we were even born….who had become a brother to me…..Preston died.

The adventures we experienced together will always be remembered. He shared in every aspect of creating our Tranquility Place until his death. We placed a memorial plaque beside his favorite RV parking space, in this place of rest he loved as we did.

There is something very special about Tranquility Place. Even my new friend Sheryl told me, "I have lived here all my life, and I never knew this place existed. It is so peaceful and calm on this hill…."

Yes, it's true.

Chapter 11

THE GATHERING HOUSE

Eventually, we knew we needed a big room for the crowds that we were already having visit us….and for other events we hoped to have. That dream came true with a beautiful building with a giant window looking eastward toward the morning sun, and big porches where people can sit and watch the sunset in the evening.

I was going to be happy to have a great big room with tables and chairs, and kitchen facilities. But Bill set the decorating tone when he began to buy furnishings and paintings in a western motif.

Soon, we had a living room setting, and the entire room had a personality. Some of those paintings had to come down later, because we found that each of us wanted to bring our family memorabilia from home. Soon, there was a Chambers gallery on one side of the huge window, and a Gilmore location on the other.

We tried several names before somebody casually mentioned it as being the Gathering House….and we knew that was the right name. Bud Thompson made a shingle to hang from the front porch eave, above the sidewalk that winds its way upward from the bathhouse.

Our Old Friends group approved of it….and so did the HOG Chapter….so much so that both groups have returned several times, and will be back. As large as it is, we had an overflow crowd at one of the HOG runs, and many people sat at outdoor tables on the porches or under the trees.

To add the icing on the cake, the property on the west and south of us came up for sale. Even though it was 200 acres, Jimmy and Vickie bought it. They thought we didn't know they were doing it for us, because we didn't want anybody to build next to our Paradise….

In the few short years since that purchase, that property has become an attraction all of its own. Cecil and Debbie put their own RV on that side of the fence, and began cutting trails through the brush and trees, and opening up areas of beauty for the rest of the family to enjoy. Jimmy and Vickie now are glad they bought it. No doubt they will have their own little home on it in the near future.

In 2005, we hosted the Chambers Family Reunion, in a 'trial run' to see how Tranquility Place and the Gathering House would work out. The test got a stamp of approval. So, while this book was in progress in June, 2006, the standard even-year reunion established this location as the site for my family to gather in years to come.

We know now why God led us here. And we know He wants us to share the joy and serenity with our family and close friends.

Chapter 12

PARTY TIME!

February 19, 2005, was Bill's and my Fifty-fifth Wedding anniversary. We decided to have a party, rather than a formal reception. We wanted this thing to be fun, and it was! But it was something we had not expected, too….an outpouring of love from our friends that will last us the rest of our lives.

Becky had moved to Kingston some time after Karlee's wedding. We worked at restoring our old relationship. When I was ill, she was the one who took me back and forth to the doctor. When she had to be out of town, I was the one who kept Marcus, took him to school and picked him up.

He adopted me as his grandma, since I was already Karlee's, Kelly's, Kenny Glen's and Angel's grandma. So it was just natural for the two of them to help me with preparations for our big event.

The invitation list included a few friends from each our social paths, who lived somewhat near-by. If we had known how it would turn out, we would have included everybody, from far and near. I don't know how that Gathering House would have held them all, but I would have been willing to push the limits to have had every last one of our loved ones there...We just didn't realize it would be such an important night.

Of course, Cecil and Debbie, Jimmy and Vickie, Billy, Denise, and Lilah were there. Kenny joined Becky and Marcus, and they had ordered a most unusual cake, with our Marriage Certificate reproduced in the icing. It was fabulous.

Other than Karlee and Jake, I had not specified that grandchildren were required to attend, but told them they could if they wanted to. Cecil Joe, Jana, Cullen and Cadence came, and so did Bobbie

Lynn and Angel. Also among our family members were Charlotte, and Veneta and Bill.

Billy seems to always be selected as the Emcee of any program, and this was no exception. We thought it would be fun and interesting for each person to tell about their relationship with us, beginning with those who had known us the longest. Boy, that was hard! When he asked those who had known us for more than 50 years, nearly the whole room stood up!

Bob and Bonnie, Pat, Mike and Frances all counted double as old family-friends before they became part of our Harley old timers....Then there were Richard and Helen, Nick and June, later additions to our HOG family.

Bud and Billie, our long-time buddies, the father-figure that kept my boys in line, later shared the camping world with us, along with Pat.

Dean and Ruby were among those who had known Bill all of his life, and me for all of our married life. Mitch counted back to the time when Bill worked for his dad at Sheppard Field, when Mitch himself was a teen-ager. He had Kay in tow....All of them had a personal interest in the development of Tranquility Place.

Then, there were those high school friends......Pug and Gerald, Paula and Wayne, Walter and Wilma, Wanda, Franklin, and, of course, Leonard and Nettie.

We were not expecting all the precious sentiments that were expressed in honoring us. It astounded and humbled us. We always knew we had the best friends and family in the world. That evening simply confirmed it.

Because we wanted people to stay late that night, we rented rooms at the Lake Texoma Lodge, for guests that couldn't be fitted into the RV's on our property, or in our house. A few went home, but most stayed. Many of them remained in the Gathering House long after Bill and I turned in for the night. I heard later that the poker games lasted until dawn….Money-less poker, let me emphasize….

I don't remember who cooked breakfast the next morning, but the party resumed. Seems to me that I remember a few guests still there for supper that night!!!!

...another damned dog...

Chapter 13

CATS DOGS BIRDS FISH

I can't imagine life without pets. They have always been an important part of my life.

I've talked about Spot, Gomer and Lightening, and my Fannie. I told about my tiny parrots that Bill brought from overseas, but I think I forgot to mention that after they were both gone, Dennis got me another one....A male we called Jose. He lived among cats and dogs for several years before he died of a disease, back before vets cared about doctoring a bird.

We had a German Shepherd watch dog for a while. He was bought for the business, and he watched as burglars cut holes in the walls, and watched them carry out thousands of dollars of tools. His sweet little foot prints were mixed with those of the culprits, so we knew they were customers who had made friends with Skipper....

So, he was retired, and came to live in our back yard.

While Bill was overseas, the boys and I were gone one day. When we came home, Skipper was not in the back yard. Our neighbor, Bart Rogers told me he had seen a man in the yard, but didn't question it

I just hope the thief stole our pet to be a Watch Dog!

Bill was still gone, and the boys wanted another pet. So, we pooled our money and bought the sweetest little screw-tail Boston terrier. His name was Chopper. We only had him a couple of months. Somebody poisoned him. It didn't make sense. He wasn't loose in the neighborhood, and he didn't bark much. In fact, he slept in the house at night. But for some cruel reason, somebody felt the need to kill him.

Gomer and Lightening were our next pets. They were best of friends. Lightening didn't have anything to do with me, until she was pregnant. Then she always became MY cat.

We allowed her to have two litters before we had her spayed. Both times, I fixed her a box in our closet. Completely uncharacteristic for a cat, she had her kittens in the box, and never moved them.

When she left the kittens alone, Gomer would run into the closet, and sit with his head hanging over the edge of the box, watching the babies. Then, when Lightening returned, he would move over and let her in the box before he ambled off. There was never any question that he was her baby-sitter.

Bea and Tinkerbelle also found their way into a previous chapter of my book, but their stories continued for many years.

When Karlee was about 7 or 8, she wanted a dog of "her own". But she wanted one just like Bea. So, we watched the ads, and finally went to see a litter of Beagles....Unfortunately, the parents were big hunting dogs....not the dainty little show-dog breed of Beagles. Bill and I started to walk away, but we were not quick enough! A puppy jumped up on Karlee, and she instantly insisted, "This is the one I want!"

To add to our dismay, she named her dog Charley. We tried to explain to her that we would always have trouble calling the dog without her thinking we were saying "Karlee". No amount of talking could change her mind. So, for the next decade, the dog came when we called our granddaughter, and our granddaughter came when we called the dog!

While Angel was living in Albuquerque, Karlee and I went out to help her move into a new apartment. She had a cat that she couldn't take to her new home. Against all instincts, I finally agreed to bring NoMore home with me....I knew Bill was going to be mad, because Tinkerbelle liked dogs.... not other cats. But Bill fell in love with NoMore, and Tinkerbelle just had to get used to him being around. It took a long time!

Bea and Charley moved to Tranquility Place with me, when I began staying for longer periods of time. Bill kept the cats at home. Then, two little kittens were born at the shop, beautiful snow white balls of fur. He brought them to me. We named them Sandy and Peanut.

I had not had those two very long when Cullen came to spend a week with me. We were out walking near the gate, when we heard a kitten meowing. Soon, this little ragamuffin came out of the brush, dirty and nearly starved. Of course, we took him to the house. His name became Hobo....

Now....with three male kittens in the house....they all decided they would not use the litter box. We had carpets at the time, and running from one spot to another to clean up after them got the best of me. I sent them back home with Bill! They now live in the barn behind our house, and are huge, healthy, happy cats. When Bill is at Tranquility Place with me, Karlee takes care of them.

I finally told Bill to bring Tinkerbelle and NoMore to me. I was afraid that Tinkerbelle would die at home alone, while he was at work. She was very old...

Charley was mean, and was a very good watch dog. So, I was never afraid while he was here. But he began to bite me, and to attack Bea, for no reason.

Even though he was younger than either Bea or Tinkerbelle, Charley got sick suddenly. Bill took him home to our vet. He was diagnosed with several fatal diseases, and the vet recommended putting him to sleep. Bill called me, and we talked it over. We knew he was hurting. I had grown up a lot since refusing to allow Pat Pasteusek to put Spot to sleep. Still, it was hard.

Little Bea was not strong enough to protect me....so, Kenny gave me his Saint Bernard, Sheena, and her year-old Black Lab offspring, Lisa. Almost immediately, a neighbor opened the gate and Lisa was gone. Several people mentioned seeing her, and she was really beautiful. So I believe she found a good home.

During a period of time when I was sick, and couldn't care for all the animals, Bill took the cats and Bea home with him, leaving me with Sheena. Bea was 18 at the time, a year younger than Tinkerbelle. She was getting very feeble and blind. He let her outside at home, and she disappeared, never to be seen again. Our hearts were broken.

Then, Kenny reclaimed another of the same Black Lab litter of Sheena's, and brought me Belle Starr. She had been abused, and was leery at first of human kindness.

Both dogs were good with Tinkerbelle and NoMore. Sheena would sit by my chair on the porch, and lay her head in my lap, as her eyes talked to me. I told her my secrets, too! That head was so huge that it completely filled my lap.

But she was not happy to stay within the confines of a 10 acre fence. That's why Kenny couldn't keep her at home…. she dug out of the yard. But who would believe that our acreage would not be big enough for her? She kept digging under the hog wire fencing that surrounds the place.

We walked the fence line and put huge rocks under the fence where she had dug, or we felt it was a possible spot for her to get out. Still, the night came when Sheena moved one of those rocks… I could call it a boulder….and under the fence she went. Belle obviously followed her.

The next morning, Belle was at the back door, traumatized. I began looking for Sheena. After giving up on our property, I got in the car, and drove down the highway. I found her, halfway between our place and the top of the hill to the west of us. She had tried to get home, but couldn't make it.

At first, I thought she had been hit by a car. But from the lack of damage to her body, and the position she was lying in, with her feet toward the bottom of the ditch, I began to question that. I called home, and Kelly came after her body.

From that day on, Belle was terrified of loud noises, especially gun shots, and I knew she had witnessed her mother being shot.

Our neighbor, Mary told other people that we had lost our Saint Bernard. Soon, she received a call telling her that the shelter at Ardmore had a Saint Bernard that we might want to adopt.

We called, and yes, they did…We drove over there to the most beautiful Humane Society we had ever seen. We were directed back to where the Saint Bernard was penned. There we saw a pathetic, tiny, starving dog with a Saint Bernard's head, cowered behind a small, perky little terrier that bounced around, begging us to take him….We had to remember we were not looking for a DOG…. We were there for that Saint Bernard. We adopted her, knowing she was almost dead.

She had not yet been spayed, so we waited for that required surgery to be done, in spite of her condition. Then I went to pick her up. A little teen-aged girl picked her up, and put her into my suburban. She was so tiny that I named her Little Lulu.

It took many weeks of loving care before Lulu would trust me, or even eat. She didn't want to get back in the car when I went home, but I finally coaxed her. I watched her as we drove through Marietta… She tensed up, and waited for me to turn toward Ardmore, thinking I was taking her back.

As we drove on west of I-35, she began to relax. Once at home in Iowa Park, she decided she must be our dog, after all. The trip back to Tranquility Place was just going home for her.

She is still a little dog for a Saint Bernard. But I don't know anybody who can pick her up! She and Belle are inseparable.

In October 2005, I went home for Homecoming. Becky and Marcus were watching Tranquility Place for me, although I had taken all my pets home.

Becky called me and said there was a scruffy dog hanging around. I told her to get rid of him…. No luck. When I returned, he met me, and Belle and Lulu, and told us we were on his property, but if we behaved, we could stay.

Belle and Lulu loved him. I tried not to….but it was cool that night, and when I saw him curled up on the porch the next morning, shivering, looking so forlorn….I fell in love.

I called Bill and told him we had another dog. The same sentence was repeated about six times…"We're not having another damned dog!!!"

When Bill came, he brought Tinkerbelle and NoMore into the house. That damned dog ran in, and they all greeted one another as if it was established that he was indeed on his own territory. Bill walked out and got on the Gator….That damned dog jumped up in his lap.

Bill's next words to me were, "Let's go get his shots, and have him fixed."

Oh….His name is Peewee. I finally have a lap dog. The first time we allowed him to spend the night in the house, he ran to the bed, dug under the covers, and headed to the foot to sleep. Well….. why not?   Damned dog!

Nobody knows what he is. His face looks like a Chihuahua, and he runs like a Whippet. So we have decided he is a Chiwhippet.

In March, 2006, Bill had gone home when I called him back. I knew twenty-one year old Tinkerbelle was dying. NoMore knew it too, and stood over her. They had become close in the past few years. The local vet had told me he had done all he could do. I didn't choose to put her to sleep.

When Bill got here, he held her until bedtime. Then we put her between us in our bed. She stretched her paw out and put it on my shoulder. I finally fell asleep. When I woke up, I knew she was gone, and woke Bill.

He buried her beneath a large sandstone, with a concrete dog standing watch over her.

Yes, we love our animals.

Bill never appreciated the wild birds until he began staying at Tranquility Place with me. Now, he recognizes nearly all of them: cardinals, chickadees, titmice, several different woodpeckers, bluebirds, and even a painted bunting….He's the one who does the feeding….except for the hummingbirds. It's my job to make the nectar and feed the swarm of about 50 hummers that entertain us the summer months. As soon as they leave, the goldfinches come by the hundreds for the winter. I even experienced a one-on-one with a bald eagle, eye to eye!

As a child, I sat for hours watching the goldfish in the tiny pond in our front yard at Wooster Mound. It was very relaxing. Now, I feed the goldfish in the pond here at my retreat from the real world. And, watching their water ballet, I'm at peace.

God gave us these creatures for a reason.

...from good stock...

Chapter 14

THE CHAMBERS FAMILY

We came from good stock. Our parents left a heritage in their wake....Among my siblings, there are gifts of music, poetry, painting, writing and even genius. These talents have been passed on to our offspring. But greater than these is valor.

I will leave Tommy's story for him to tell in his own book.

Our sister, Roberta, was not only more beautiful than any movie star, she had guts. Yes, she was an Army Nurse. But not just any army nurse. She served on the front lines of battle, in the evacuation hospitals that received the wounded just as they were found on the fields. It was her job to separate the living from the dead, and patch the survivors to be shipped to safer locations for treatment. There was no glamour in the job.

On a lighter note, I need to insert a story here: When I was about 5 or 6 years old, there was a rule in our house that the children did not climb the ladder to the attic. The reason was the same as today.... you have to walk on the rafters, or go through the ceiling....

The ladder was in the big walk-through closet that served for not only clothing and bedding, but also as a pantry for the jars of canned foods that Mama put up. [Tin cans were few and far between back then. The only ones I remember held pork and beans.....]

That ladder was a temptation that finally got the best of us.

I've told you that Tommy was a good brother. But I left out that he could be diabolical sometimes. Well, this particular time, he kept on begging Charlotte and me to go up into the attic until we finally followed him up the ladder.

As soon as I had been pulled through the scuttle hole, Tommy leaned over and yelled, "MAMA! Guess where WE ARE!!!!" Then he jumped to the floor and ran, leaving Charlotte and me on our own! Charlotte raced down the ladder as quickly as she could, and still caught a few swats on the way down. But I was slow. I got the spanking of my life! I'm still mad at Tommy for that!

There is much more to the Chambers Family than those siblings and other relatives mentioned in connection to some part of my book. Oh, yes, I had an attachment to all my nieces and nephews while I was growing up, and those who were born during the same years as my sons. Every one of them is very dear to me.

The memories I have of each are not connected to any of the events recorded in the previous chapters. In fact, there are few 'one-on-one' contacts with them that created material for my book. That isn't to say we never talked. If I had asked each for a memory, I doubt they could pinpoint any one thing, either. But I know they love me. Well, I think so, anyway.....

Joetta was just four years younger than me, and we played together. Yet my strongest memories of her are as an adult. My favorite is one that Bill and our boys also recall with a great deal of enjoyment.

Sometime in the 1960's, our family was in Powell to visit Lillie, and the rest of the family there. Joetta and Buzz invited us over for a cook-out. She was in charge of barbequing the chicken. She forgot it a bit too long. It was just a wee bit overdone. Well, maybe a little more than that. Okay, so it was actually cremated.... Charcoal ....

Anybody else would have thrown it away, and served sandwiches. And the meal would have been quickly forgotten.

Without batting an eyelash, Joetta put that black carcass on the table, as if that was exactly the way she planned to serve it!

The meal was filled with peals of laughter. That one event has been the source of many jokes and memories for the past 40 years. That's the way I will always remember her. She died in 1998.

There have been many deaths among our individual families. Berry Lee Jr. was killed in a truck accident in 1982. I had not had a lot of personal contact with him as an adult, but Bill and I remember a great visit we had with him in Worland, while he was married to Jane.

As a very young teen-ager, I stayed with Nina when Keith was born. So I always felt like he belonged to me. We spent a lot of time together, over the years. My sons especially remember those race cars on trailers that they sometimes found in our driveway. Naturally, their friends also gathered around. Keith died in 1989.

Pam lived in Wichita Falls after the 1979 tornado long enough for the two of us to become close. Her husband was in charge of the federal funding of the rebuilding. She spent a lot of time at our house. Pam died in 1991.

Dorothy's first husband, Jerry Van Wagoner, and his father died together when their snowmobiles broke through ice on a lake in 1973, when she was just 22 years old.

Charlotte had a precious little girl named Cindy, a little younger than Richard. When Roger was a tiny baby, Cindy was suddenly taken without warning.

In my own family, we also lost Kenny's step-daughter Jolynn, and his second wife, Linda.

Each of my sisters have lost spouses. Yet, each of them made a new life, and that's as it should be.

Now, back to a bit of levity....I have a favorite story about Roger.....and I'm going to tell it one more time!

Charlotte had left Russell, Richard and Roger with me while she was tending to legal problems at home. Roger came into the kitchen one morning, and announced, "I can't pind my chues!"

"You can't find your shoes?" I asked.

"No, I can't pind my chues," he repeated.

"Where did you leave them when you took them off?"

"In de baffwoom"

"Well, go look in the bathroom."

Roger marched off, and quickly returned with a shoe in each hand. "Oh! Here dey are!" He said, "I tot dey wus somepace where I couldn' pind dem!!!"

Oh! Lets talk about it one more time....The 18th of November, 2006, sister Lillie turned 97 years old....

Chapter 15

FORGOTTEN STORIES

As soon as I finished the first part of my book, I realized I had forgotten many stories. This chapter will include all the things that failed to make it into their right place in my book....

Such as the introduction of G.W. Poole, and his wife, Lucy, into our lives........

I can't even remember what year it began, but it was in the 1970's. A stranger brought his truck to the shop, after hours. That was in the days before Bill and the boys found out they didn't have to be available 24 hours a day. Anyway. Jimmy had the man pull into the mechanic shop. It was a cold day, so he closed the overhead door behind the truck. As Jimmy worked on the engine, somehow it kicked into reverse....

Yep! Backwards it went right through that door, tearing it off, but more importantly, damaging the man's truck. Jimmy couldn't believe it had happened. Above all, he couldn't believe that the man was saying, "That's okay. Don't worry about it. I know you will fix it."

We waited for months for a lawsuit that never happened. And one of those people who are just too good to be true...but was absolutely true....G.W. came into our lives, not only as a customer, but as a family friend from that day on.

His home was in Florida, and his route ran from Miami to Denver. He picked up plants in Miami, and sold them to nurseries.

We knew Lucy only by phone conversations for years, before we met her face to face. But we loved her.

G.W. had created deep friendships all across the country, and we were just fortunate to have become one of them. Each time he came through, he would bring me one of those plants, whatever his load happened to be. I would tell him that I just could not raise anything! But the last one, I put in the Gathering House, and it is still beautiful. I could take credit, but I believe it's the tranquil setting that keeps it alive!

In later years, Lucy developed kidney cancer....yes, the same cancer I had overcome. I encouraged both of them, using my own survival as an example of hope.

In 2004, Bill and I drove down to Orlando, and spent several days with G.W. and Lucy. We met their kids, and had a wonderful time. We went to a zoo, and I bought a pink flamingo to go on my pond. Lucy was tired and had sat down on a bench to wait. When she saw my flamingo, she had to have one. I ran back to the shop, and got the very last one for her.

I wish I could say that Lucy made it, too. But she died in 2005.

G. W. is still driving his truck, not ready to retire. He recently bought another home in Denver, so he has a place to live at both ends of his route.

Then there's a terrific tale that took place when Mike and Frances got married....I don't remember why I was alone at the wedding, but after the ceremony, I rushed out. I was half-way across the parking lot when I heard Preston yelling at me to wait. I turned around, and saw one of his brothers, [no mistaking the family resemblance] rushing toward me with his arms outstretched for a hug. I soon learned that the brother I was embracing was Glenn Leath.

Glenn began talking rapidly, trying to get it all in, "Oh! I'm so glad to see you! Do you remember when your mama and daddy moved to New Mexico, and that time we all came out to see you? And Lillie took all of us for rides on the horse....And we...."

I hated to break in on him, but I finally said, "No, Glenn. I don't remember.......I wasn't born yet!!!!"

We all broke into laughter, and he continued the stories of what my older siblings and his did during that visit.

It didn't matter. I was still one of those Chambers kids.

Forgotten stories must include deaths that I omitted in the right places. As I go back over the chapters I've written, and see the names of dear friends, I realize that I have lost many over the years. Joyce Brittain Williams and Billie Faye Smith both died much too young.

Our precious Laurie, James' wife, the girl who endeared herself to all of us, fought a hard fight against cancer before she died in about 1990. We were honored to be with her just two days before. Her greatest regret was leaving their children, Scott, Ben and baby Patty. I think she knows they all grew into terrific young adults.

Then, there was Ruth Vaughan, Dennis's mother, and our very dear friend. She died in January, 1999. The memories we shared will live with our families from now on.

A few years later, her brother, Cecil Carey, died. Bill and I failed to get the message in time to go to his service.

Although Hershel and I battled at times, the close friendship with him and Ginny still existed. We were grieved many years ago when we learned that Harry Dean had died at a young age.

Most recently, we lost our young friend, Matthew Wallace, Corliss's son who had worked with me at the cemetery.

Not all loss of friends happens because of death. Among the chapters of Book II, I talked about our relationship with Dick and Ann Wooldridge. For some unknown reason, in more recent years, they cut the communications. We tried to find out why, and revive the friendship, to no avail. Finally, we just gave up.

During the year of 2006, Dennis told us he had heard through Dick Yockey, that Ann had died some time ago. We will never understand why that precious friendship ended. We can't even find Dick, now. That is the only deep relationship that we ever lost in such a painful way.

Helen recently sent me an article she prepared for the HOG newsletter. That reminded me of a story I need to tell about our ride to Milwaukee for the 90th Harley Davidson anniversary, over 10 years ago. I don't remember exactly who rode in our group, but there was a bunch of us. That was the only time I got tired of being in a crowd of motorcycles....We had to stay on the Illinois side of the border, some 50 miles from the city. Each morning, we became another dot in the pattern of HOGs, riding handle-bar to handle-bar, bumper to bumper, all the way into the fair grounds of Milwaukee.

It was also the first time I witnessed rudeness among Harley riders. The tours involved buses, and the planning had gone awry… the waiting stretched into hours at times. Then some cute young things and ugly burly brutes would race from half a block, and push themselves in ahead of the more polite senior citizens.

Finally, I got mad, and decided to do some bullying of my own. The next guy that tried to push us back got an umbrella in his ribs. We got on, and all of a sudden, there was respect in the eyes of observers.

During one period of free time, Richard and Helen, Bill, Karlee and I took advantage of our motel being near a giant mall…. actually the Chicago mall…can't remember the name….a long way out of Chicago. We parked our cycles adjacent to the Handicapped spaces, just across the crosswalk from the main entrance. We may have been inside for 15 or 20 minutes before we decided that was not our cup of tea.

When we came out, Richard's cycle was gone! We couldn't believe it. Right there under the security cameras. We decided, and still believe that the mall security officers were involved in the ring that stole hundreds of cycles that weekend. We learned they were immediately put on a ship in the port of Lake Michigan.

Bill shuttled us back to the motel, and Richard began calling all the necessary places. Not only did they lose their cycle, but their tour pack and saddle bags were full, as well. Helen and their daughter Robbie took a plane home. Richard rode Robbie's cycle.

I must say, all the other events were much more fun!!!!

Oh yes! Another motorcycling friendship that I failed to record earlier developed from one of our supper runs to Quanah, Texas, many years ago….The group had left the Harley shop as usual that Saturday night, but Vickie stayed behind to catch up on some chores.We had not been gone long when a couple and her mother stopped by in their side-car rig.

Vickie visited with them long enough to learn that they lived in Alaska, and often came down to the lower 48 states, where they kept their motorcycle stored. They were just touring the country, and happened by at that moment. Vickie told them that our Saturday Night Supper Run group had just left. She gave them directions to the restaurant where we would be, and saw them off.

That's how we met Fred and Mae Oelhert and her mother, Inez. They sat at the table with Bill and me, and Karlee, who was riding in our side car. We had enough in common to keep the conversation going! When Bill described something Jimmy had done to make our cycle easier to steer, Fred asked Jimmy if he could do the same on his cycle. Jimmy told him if he wanted to stay around until Monday, he could work on it then. Bill and I invited them to use our RV for the weekend, and so they back-tracked and spent the weekend with us.

That was the beginning of a warm friendship between us, and some later visits. We tried to arrange a visit to their home in Anchorage, but it just never happened.

After Bill and I found our Tranquility Place, I was telling Mae about it by telephone. When she learned where it was, she almost fainted. She has relatives in Kingston, and friends in Lebanon. So it was established that they would soon be our guests again. As of the writing of this book, that hasn't happened either. But they know the invitation is open.

I almost forgot another Kingston connection: My 'nephew-in-law' Buzz Larsen remarried. I guess that makes Pat my 'niece-in-law'....Whatever! We're friends.

Pat fell off her bar stool when I told her about our Oklahoma retreat. Kingston is her birthplace, and her relatives are still here. We actually know a couple of young men who are children of her cousins!

In the summer of 2006, the Weilers visited Tranquility Place for the first time. During their stay, they noticed that we didn't have a flag pole on the grounds. After they returned home, we received a beautiful pole, complete with flag, ready to be erected.

Weiler thought it belonged out in the open area to the east of the Gathering House. But Martha insisted it should be out in the front of our house, so we could see it as we sat on the front porch. You know of course, whose choice we honored….. Sorry, Weiler!

Anyway, that proud flag adds the needed touch to our home. Later, a plaque arrived, to be placed at the base of the flag. It reads, "God bless America….and the Gilmores…..from the Weilers."

These people love to give gifts, and I love to take them! One more was sent to put in the Gathering House, after they saw the décor. It was an 'antique' globe….at least, antiquated as far as countries go! Weiler said it had been with him all his adult life. Christmas, 2005, Martha bought him a new globe….a state-of-the-art computerized model. And they both wanted us to have the old one.

This gesture stirred memories of another globe in our past. Below is a copy of the e-mail I sent to them about the first globe:

> "Okay, I promised to tell you a story……Once upon a time……living in a motel unit in Twin Falls, Idaho with three little pigs…Papa Hog had a bad habit of going to auctions, which in itself doesn't sound unreasonable. Except he thought he had an obligation to bid on every item, regardless of purpose, size or cost.
>
> One day, he came home with a HUGE coffee table that would serve a Great Room today…..and a HUGE globe, on a stand yet!
>
> The Sow was not thrilled, considering the fact that keeping the items would require giving up sleeping space, and packing them into their vehicle to move would mean leaving the little pigs behind…
>
> The very next day, a friend kindly took them, and the Sow didn't even have to pay her, which was a damned good deal.
>
> The characters in this story are fictionally fiction, and any resemblance to living humans is purely intentional.
>
> Are you sleepy yet? If not, I'll bet I can think of a few more stories…."

By the way, I wonder what Ann did with that table and globe…

Chapter 16

MY GRANDCHILDREN

I have never been one of those old biddy's that carry pictures around, and capture whoever is available to show every pose of every day of a grandchild's life...Everybody knows that mine are the most beautiful of all, and after seeing them, what am I supposed to say to my friends, when they push that album in front of me "Ohhh.....that sure is a baby!!!!"

Okay, so I don't carry them in my wallet. I carry them in my heart.....every last one of them!

There's no doubt that I failed to be the grandmother I wanted to be, just as surely as I failed as a mother. But somehow I believe that all of them have taken away some good memories of Grandma's house.

They are all grown up now, except for Lilah, and the great-grandkids. I still have some time to play with the young ones. But for the most part, my grandchildren have outgrown me. I don't say that as a ploy for attention. I say it because it is a fact of life, a natural process, just as true as when my boys outgrew me, and just as heart-wrenching to see them facing life on their own.

Leonard recently told us "You are so fortunate. I know you have had lots of problems with your grandchildren, and really, ours haven't given us any trouble. But when I see yours with you, the way they hug you, and kiss you, and tell you they love you, I think I'd rather have the problems, if ours would just pay attention to us, and show us half as much love."

Yes, there are problems. But yes, there is love, unquestionably. I have learned to be concerned, but not to worry about my grandchildren. I survived. They will, too. My children have lost their way, just as I did. They will find the right path again, just as

I did. My thoughts and prayers will always follow them. They will hit the depths of despair, and come out on top.

They are my children......my grandchildren.....my great-grandchildren. I refuse to give up on them.

Chapter 17

SILVER FRIENDS

When we were kids, one of the rounds we sang in school went like this: Make new friends, but keep the old. One is silver, and the other, gold.

I have a treasure chest full of gold friends from my first seventy years on Earth. Since finding Tranquility Place, I have not really looked for new friends. I enjoy my solitude, when Bill is at home, and I'm alone. Yet I've managed to find a purse full of silver the past few years.

First of all, I looked up one day, and saw neighbors working on the fence that separated our property. I strolled over and met Sheryl and Albert Lee Self. When Bill came up, we became better acquainted, and spent a lot of quality time with them. They sold their place, and moved to a gated community near the State Park Lodge. With both of us occupied, we just let communications slide. But, we consider them to be our good friends, and we hope to see them again soon.

Then there was Mary Cook, who lived across the road from us. Her husband, Carl, died the first year we had our place, so she was alone. Her son, Doug Gallaway, often came to see her, and as the months passed, we did indeed become good friends. It was Mary who took care of me when I was burned. We have really missed her, since she moved to be near her kids.

Sheryl introduced me to Bobbie Pierce, at Yard Designs in Kingston. As time passed, Bobbie and her boyfriend, Bert, and her daddy, Gene Day, have become very dear to all my family. It's a relationship that will continue through the years.

There are a number of casual friendships made since coming to Tranquility Place that we enjoy. Time may bring others, but we are rich with the love of these few selected Silver Friends.

Chapter 18

THINGS I HAVE LEARNED

Periodically, an e-mail is passed around that lists the things learned in life. The list changes with the number of times it is forwarded.

One of them says "I have learned that you can't make somebody love you. All you can do is stalk them until they give in."

Well, in fact, I have learned that you can't even make a person like you, no matter how hard you try....Some personalities just clash. So, give it up already!!!! Get on with life!

There are other lessons I have learned, and to the best of my knowledge, this list is original and confined to me. It's in no particular order....just listed as I thought of the items....

I have learned how to use the computer to my own satisfaction and for my own purposes. The rest doesn't matter.

I have learned that my brother DOES love me!

I have learned that my mouth still needs to be washed out with soap.

I have learned that there are two kinds of people in life... those that betray you with a vengeance.....and those who betray you with regret, and ask for forgiveness. I've learned that when you are asked for forgiveness, you have to give it.

I have learned that I do have a creative mind. The problem is, I'm asleep at the time, and can't remember my inventions after I wake up.

I have learned that, no matter how many friends I have, I can't afford to lose one.

I have learned that I have to have a pen and paper beside my bathtub, because I do my best thinking while bathing.

I have learned that there are people who just let life go right on by as it will, rather than to make a decision of their own.

I have learned that old people fall in love just as passionately as young people, and their hearts get broken just as badly.

I have learned that it's impossible to maintain a relationship with a person who has no sense of humor.

I have learned to be very careful about the people I trust as critics. A person who cannot do what you do is not qualified to tell you how to do it....

I have learned that it's easy to say "I don't worry about getting old and wrinkled," when you are young and well-stacked.

I have learned that I must keep learning, even though I know it all.....

I have learned that true friends can disagree openly, and say so without anger. As Helen told me, "If we agreed on everything, it would be very dull. I still love you.....

Chapter 19

WHAT'S IN A NAME?

The title of this book is _The Many Lives of Maryanne_. I like the name, Maryanne. I'm glad that's what my mama named me. I think she named all her children beautiful names. Some of them didn't like their names. But I like mine.

When I have to tell my name, for whatever reason, I emphasize, "It's Maryanne. One word. M-a-r-y-a-n-n-e." Invariably, the person who has just been told my name will ask, "And what is your address, Mary?"

I do believe you have just learned the root of my reputation for being sensitive and difficult! My name is not Mary.

It is not Anne. Only my mother-in-law called me Anne. She could call me anything she wanted to…..and I'm sure she did!

A few other people are allowed to call me by a nickname, or pet name. They know who they are. Others can make my name sound like music.

So, just who is this Maryanne with the many lives?
I'm many personalities to many people.

I'm Baby Sister…. as my siblings have now begun to call me. To them, I will always be the baby.

I'm Mama. I'm Mom. I'm Grandma. I'm Great-grandma.
I'm Aunt Maryanne. I'm Mama Maryanne.
I'm a sincere friend to those who call me Friend.

I'm that young teen-ager that played with nieces and nephews who were almost my age.

I'm the new girl on the stairs at school, smiling at a boy below.

Who knows? I might be a fantasy to some old codger! Truth is, I'm old. I'm fat. I'm wrinkled. But I'm young and beautiful to a 90 year old!!!!

I'm the old woman who just blew the head off of a rattlesnake with my 38 Special from 26' away.....Yep! I have now been dubbed Granny Oakley.....so don't mess with me!

I've always been Honey to Bill, even in the worst of times.

Above all, I'm me......Maryanne....I'm just me. I'm all the things that life has made me, good, bad, or indifferent. I pray that Forgiveness has destroyed Bitterness in me. I'll have to live a lot longer to claim Wisdom.

I am whoever I happen to be to the person reading my book.

Chapter 20

LOOKING FORWARD

I called Bill at home, and told him I was down to the last chapter of my book, and I didn't know how to end it. He said, "Don't worry. You will do just fine."   Hummm…

It's been a hard life. It's been a wonderful life. It's still hard. It's still wonderful. The pain is there. But it will never be the focus of my life. I prefer to wear rose-colored glasses, and not see the real world. Or maybe I am seeing the real world…..the one God created, the way He meant for it to be.   I'm looking forward.

I have something to say, then we are not going talk about it any more…. In February, 2007, I will be 75 years old……..

THE BEGINNING

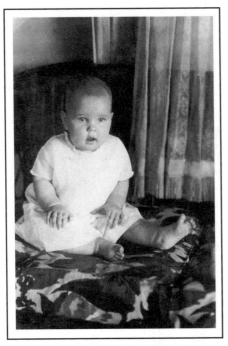

I've still got it....it's just a little lower!

Fifty-fifth

Anniversary

TO BE CONTINUED.....